A Chapter of
TALMUD

Bava Metzia – Chapter Ten
"A House and Its Upper Floor"
Pages 116b–119a

LAWRENCE F. LAYFER

DEVORA
PUBLISHING

מסורה
הש"ס

הבית והעלייה פרק עשירי בבא מציעא

232

עין משפט
נר מצוה

A Chapter of Talmud: Bava Metzia – Chapter 10
Published by Devora Publishing Company
Text Copyright © 2008 by Lawrence F. Layfer

Cover and Book Design: **Benjie Herskowitz**
Editorial and Production Manager: **Daniella Barak**
Editor: **Meshulam Gotlieb**

Hard Cover ISBN: 978-1-934440-06-3
E-mail: publisher@devorapublishing.com
Website: www.devorapublishing.com

Printed in Israel

This book is dedicated
to my father, his father, and especially to my paternal
great-grandfather, Rabbi Ephraim, for whom I am named
and whom I have always had in mind while writing;
to my wife and children, Linda, David, Lisa, and Laura,
for listening more than anyone should have to;
to my mother and brother, Betty and Barry;
and to the man in the desert, Steve Geller.

CONTENTS

ACKNOWLEDGMENTS

Many people contributed to the genesis and writing of this book, and I would like to express my deepest gratitude to them: to Rabbi Shlomo Simon for years of patiently leading me through vast tracts of Talmud and for his help translating the Talmudic passages in this book; to Rabbi William Frankel for sharing his insights on the Talmud as a vehicle for seeing each human being as created in the image of God; to the *Am Yisrael* Talmud class for showing up every week to listen and to share; to Dr. Elliot Lefkovitz for his manuscript review; to Rabbi Debra Newman-Kamin and Mrs. Leah Polin for enabling me to find my voice; to Joseph Aaron and Pauline Yearwood for providing such a wonderful writing venue these many years; to Meshulam Gotlieb, my editor, for all his help; to my publisher, Yaacov Peterseil, for the opportunity; and to Rabbi Joel Lehrfield and Rabbi Joseph Gross for getting me started.

PROLOGUE

Many students of the Talmud, both veteran talmudists and beginners, are overwhelmed by the vastness and complexity of its discussions. Therefore, in this book I have attempted to show how the Rabbis of the *Mishnah* and the *Gemara* think their way through a topic. I have done this by analyzing and clarifying the material found in a single, brief, three-page, Talmud chapter found at the end of tractate *Bava Metzia*. Aimed at readers who have never opened a volume of Talmud before, this book provides a clear, flowing summary in English of what the Mishnah and Gemara have to say, concerning this one complete, but short, chapter. Rather than giving a historical review of the Talmud's development, focusing on the methodology of Talmudic interpretation, or offering biographical sketches of the Rabbis whose commentaries fill the Gemara, this book will directly take you, the reader, for a "swim in the sea of the Talmud." With translations and commentaries explaining and summarizing the Mishnah and Gemara as a guide, you need never feel out of your depth. By the end of this book, we hope you will be pleasantly surprised to find that you have now studied and understood an entire chapter of Talmud. You will then have joined the long line of receivers and transmitters of the Oral Law.

מסורה
הש"ס

הבית והעלייה פרק עשירי בבא מציעא

עין משפט
נר מצוה

232

הבית והעלייה

הבית והעלייה של שנים · מכן שני אחים שחלקו אחד נפל בים
ואחד נפל עליו שעל גביו והאבנים של מעות הבית מן
מקרית הבית התחתונה שהיא קרקעיתה על עליה ולמעלה של
שלוין ורומא וגלמטה של התחתן · שעניה תולקים · הכל לפ (א) הנטיה
"שהאחד הוא נטיה מחכירו ואבניו
ועפרו מרובה מטל פניהו תולקים
לפי שאין ניכר איזו אבנים של עלין
ואיזו אבנים של התחתן : מואם אלו
אבנים רחויות והשחכר · אם יש
אבנים שטוריה של לבנים זה אומר
שלימות שלי חה אומר שלימות שלי
מואן אלו אבנים רחויות והשחכר
אם של עלין אם של התחתן והכל
מטרו ונפל המפלה שאם נחבט הבית
יש לזה שהתחתונת ופבניו ולכך
גפלה "הבית ואם נחבט כמותל
פמגומותה של מותל נפלו גהל וגפל

הבית "והעלייה של שנים שנפלו שניהם
חולקין בעצים ובאבנים ובעפר וראין
אלו אבנים העשויות להשתבר אם היה ארד
מכן מביר מקצת אבני נוטל ועולות לו מן
החשבון : **גמ'** מדקתני רואן מכלל ידאיכא
למיקם עלידו אי בחבסא נפל או בחבסא
נפיל או דכי רישא אמאי חולקין נחזי אי
בחבסא נפל עלירתא איתבור לא בחבסא
נפל תתירתא איתבור לא צריכא דנפיל
בליליא וליחזינהו בצפרא דפנינדר וליחזי מאן
פנינהו ולישיליה דפנינדר בני רשת הרבים
דאזיל לעלמא וליחזי ברשת דבאתרבן וליהדי
איך הנוינא מחבירו עלי דבראיה לא

הבית והעלייה: ול'יחן כרסות למאן קיימי ט' · ולי'ח דהבא
פשיעא ליה לפירי בנפל לרשות דהר מייים שבן רגלות
הוא שאינ טפל כלמטום בשה וברים בבא כתרא (רף ד') פריך
פשיעא דלא נפל הכותל דהוי של שניהם ומטני לא גריכא דנפל
לרשות דחר ויל משום דאוק' לה
הכא למועתים כשל זה מטו כשל זה
פריך התם פשיעא דהוה תמוטת ליה
לא הקמה דוגיא דהכא בנמניע לפניה
נכמתך ועור דהם (נ) פריך מתוך
הטענא דפיר פריך פשיעא
ל'יטא כירי היובתא דרי דאמר
פטור ולא'ג'ע נעטמא דר'י
משום דאוק' ממומ בחוק מחיים
והא דקי'מנאקיימי מכחל לו בחמר
שאינ של שניהם שאין התחבד מותו
יותר מחבירו מ"מ כהם מפ'כ מותק
שחו יורעין שמו שלו לגך פריך
מ'י ושד רבף' הטולל (דף כד) כהם
ואם דבל מתן שאון נשול בהם

INTRODUCTION

The Talmud has its roots in the Oral Law. When Moses received the Written Law, the Torah, on Mount Sinai, tradition teaches us that he spent the next forty days discussing the specifics of each law with God. The lessons Moses learned form the basis of the Oral Law. The image of God and Moses toiling day and night to determine how to apply the written Torah to everyday situations is still re-enacted in every house of study today. In questioning God regarding the permutations and ramifications of the Written Law during his stay on Mount Sinai, Moses created the paradigm for studying the Talmud. Indeed, just as case law is necessary to apply the United States of America's Constitution to everyday situations, so too the Oral Law is necessary to understand and apply the Written Law, the Torah, to daily life.

After descending from Mount Sinai, Moses gave the Written Law to the Israelites, and also shared the Oral Law with them. For forty years he carefully oversaw their studies as they discussed the Oral Law amongst themselves, studying it and learning it in pairs or in groups. After Moses's death, a combination of forgetfulness among the scholars and, with the passage of time, the need to apply the law to novel situations led to disputes. These escalated into the many discussions and arguments that fill the pages of the Talmud.

Until Roman times, the Oral Law remained true to its name, as it was transmitted orally from master to student. When Roman persecution threatened the Jews' ability to continue to transmit the Oral Law to a new generation of scholars, Rabbi Yehudah HaNasi

11

(Rabbi Judah the Prince) issued a halachic (legal) ruling permitting the collection, redaction and editing of a corpus of oral laws into written form. This collection was later known as the Mishnah. Conceived as an outline of the Oral Law, this memory aid could not stand by itself. A master teacher, skilled in the Oral Law, was still necessary to elucidate the Mishnah and transmit the Oral Law. For this reason, several centuries later when the Rabbis again feared for the successful transmission of the Oral Law to future generations, a further documentation of the rabbinic arguments, this time with copious detail, was added. This collection became known as the Gemara.

As time passed, stories and other folk messages, as well as ethical teachings, were also included in the Gemara. Since at the time there were two major centers of Jewish life and scholarship, two compilations composed of the Mishnah and its attendant Gemara were actually composed: the Jerusalem Talmud in Israel, and the Babylonian Talmud in Babylon. Predictably, the Jerusalem Talmud contains more material concerning the Israeli reality and its Sages while the Babylonian Talmud has a more Diaspora focus. We will be concentrating our study on the Babylonian Talmud, for it rapidly became the most significant work of Oral Law for the Jewish people.

There is a majestic and mystical quality to the study of Talmud, even when the Sages discuss the most secular subjects. Any reader, at any stage of learning, can experience this sensation. Entering into a debate with the Talmudic sages, arguing along with the classical commentators over the meaning of a text, debating the text's applicability to a particular situation create a sense of kinship with our predecessors and a bridge linking us to our successors.

It is said that when we pray, we are talking to God, but that when we study – if we listen closely – we can hear God talking to us. In describing his experience of studying the Gemara, Rabbi J. B. Soloveitchik noted that while he was not a kabbalist or a mystic, when studying Gemara he felt as if the Holy One, blessed be He, was standing behind him, placing His hand on his shoulder, looking into the Gemara, and asking, "What are you studying here?"

The Mishnah has sixty-three tractates. These are divided into six orders: *Zera'im* (Seeds), *Mo'ed* (Festival Days), *Nashim* (Women), *Nezikin* (Damages), *Kodashim* (Holy Things), and *Toharot* (Purities). Our tractate, *Bava Metzia*, is part of the order named *Nezikin*. While the Mishnah is written in Hebrew, the Gemara is written in the language spoken by the Jews of its time, Aramaic. The Aramaic title for our tractate, *Bava Metzia*, means "Middle Gate." It is the second volume in a trilogy of three tractates that may at one point have made up one, very lengthy tractate named "Damages." The other two tractates are named *Bava Kamma* (The First Gate) and *Bava Batra* (The Last Gate). As the name of the order, *Damages*, implies, much of these three tractates deals with responsibility for interactions between people and/or their property, both in public (business) and private (personal) settings. Issues such as loan agreements, contracts, employer-employee relationships, guardianship, lost objects, fraud and abuse, just weights and measures, and monetary policy are mixed with stories of the lives and morality of the Rabbis found in the tractates.

Our chapter, the tenth and final chapter of *Bava Metzia*, is entitled "A House and Its Upper Floor" based upon the opening words of the chapter. It has as its major focus some of the issues surrounding jointly owned property, landlord-tenant relationships, building codes, and employment agreements. Why choose this mundane and secular chapter to introduce the Talmud? First, the chapter is short, lending itself to easy completion by a first-time reader. Second, considering Talmudic arguments in relatively familiar situations allows us to focus upon the logic of the arguments, rather than upon the novelty of the subject. Third, no part of the Talmud has precedence over another: all are equally important in God's eyes. Fourth, and perhaps most important, there is something very special about finding the sacred in the most abjectly secular, human concerns and encounters.

We spend most of our lives dealing with the mundane activities of daily living. In these situations, overcome with self-interest and prepared for battle, we are most at risk of failing to sanctify common human interactions. We must remind ourselves that the person sitting across from us at the table is created in God's image, and that our personal and business dealings with him or her must reflect this. As Rabbi Israel Salanter, the eighteenth-century founder of the Musar Movement, is reputed to have said: "A person should be more concerned with spiritual than with material matters, but another person's material welfare is my spiritual concern."

After explaining and summarizing each mishnah and its accompanying Gemara in this book, I have added brief essays, entitled "Ethical Insights," that will enable you to explore in greater detail an ethical matter raised by our Gemara in the course of its discussion.

Now, let us begin learning!

Part One:
THE MISHNAH WITH COMMENTARY

All Talmudic discussions begin with the Mishnah. Redacted and edited by Rabbi Yehudah HaNasi in the second century of the Common Era, the Mishnah is the first written instance of the Oral Law and, as such, is the oldest of the Talmudic writings. Designed as a memory aid so that the Oral Law would not be forgotten, the word "mishnah" literally means "to repeat" or "to teach." The Rabbis believed that repetition leads to memorization and enhanced understanding.

For a Gemara student, the Mishnah provides both a brief, schematic introduction to the contents in any given chapter and a welcome haven, allowing the student to refocus at any time on the essentials of the ongoing discussion as he or she sails through what can sometimes feel like the directionless waters of the Gemara. In fact, some students love the Mishnah – its brevity and its clarity – so much that they are content to study it alone, deciding it is enough to give them a feel for the basics of Jewish law. Several classical commentaries and many contemporary study groups confine themselves to exclusively studying this part of the Talmud.

Even for those wishing to study the Talmud in its entirety, both the Mishnah and its accompanying Gemara, first learning the Mishnah affords the opportunity of getting an overview of the material to be studied in any particular chapter. This is a good idea, for then, even before beginning to study the Gemara, you become familiar with the types of issues and legal discussions coming up in the Gemara. Therefore, I will begin this book by offering a fairly literal translation of and my own basic commentary upon each of the six mishnahs found in our chapter. The Mishnah translation, like the translation of the Gemara, is a running translation incorporating a literal rendering of the Hebrew or Aramaic texts, in bold-face and my parenthetical, non-literal interpolations designed to aid the reader. During the course of the book, as we study the Gemara together, I recommend that you briefly review each mishnah again, before studying its accompanying Gemara.

MISHNAH ONE: *A House Collapses*

(In this first case) **a house (lower story) and an upper story belonging to two people collapsed. The two owners split the wood, the stones, and the mortar. And we (the court) determine which stones are likely to have broken. If one of them recognizes some of his stones, he takes them, but they count for him as part of his reckoning.**

The mishnah deals with a case where two individuals, partners or – according to the great Talmudic commentator Rashi – brothers who inherited the property from their father, own a two-story building. One owner lives on the ground floor and owns that part of the building; the other lives on the second story and owns that part of the building. The building collapses, and the mishnah teaches them how to divide the rubble: they split all the bricks and all the wood – broken or whole – and the mortar in a proportional fashion. If the way in which the house collapsed testifies to the ownership of a specific part of the rubble, the court distributes it accordingly. If one of the owners identifies some of the materials as his own, for instance, some of the unbroken bricks, he may take them. However, they will be subtracted from his portion of the divided assets. The two owners do not split the assets equally, fifty-fifty, but rather proportionally; thus, if the ground- floor apartment was larger than the second-story one, its owner would receive a proportionally larger portion of the split. At first glance, the process delineated by the mishnah seems to be a just and logical way of dividing these assets. The Gemara will explore some of the difficulties that arise in applying these principles.

MISHNAH TWO: *A Hole in the Floor*

(In the case of) a house (ground floor) **with an upper story** (second floor), **the upper story's** (floor partially) **caved in** (creating an open hole between the two dwellings), **and the owner of the building** (who lives on the ground floor) **does not want to fix it. The occupant of the upper story** (a renter) **may descend and live downstairs until he** (the building's owner) **repairs the second story's floor. Rabbi Yose says that the** (building's owner, living on the) **lower** (floor) **provides** (the material for the part of) **the ceiling** (that acts as a foundation for repairing the hole in the upstairs floor) **and the upper** (floor occupant, the renter) **provides the plaster** (to cover the foundation provided by the owner).

The previous case involved two owners, one owning the ground-floor apartment and the other owning the second-story apartment. The Rabbis usually understand this current case to be between the building's owner, who lives on the ground floor, and a tenant who rented the upper floor. The mishnah quite literally teaches that if the second-story apartment is made unlivable because its floor partially caved in, the building's owner must either repair the hole or allow the tenant to move into the ground-floor apartment with him until repairs are made. The ruling offered by the Rabbis in the first half of the mishnah implies that the building's owner is completely responsible for the cost of materials and labor needed to fix the hole. Rabbi Yose disagrees with this, noting that the repair costs should be divided between the owner and his tenant. Rabbi Yose feels that the floor/ceiling structure is composed of two parts: the actual ceiling, which separates the first and second stories, and a plaster coating that covers the ceiling upon which the tenant walks. He believes that while the owner should supply the basic materials for the repair, the tenant should supply the plaster coating that overlays the ceiling foundation. Is the plaster merely a convenient way for the tenant to gain a smooth floor, therefore, becoming his responsibility, or is the plaster an integral part of the ceiling/floor structure, in which case the building's owner should also pay for this part of the repair?

MISHNAH THREE: *Upon Whom Does the Obligation Fall to Rebuild a Collapsed House?*

(In the case where) **the house (ground floor) and the (attached) upper story, belonging to two (people), collapsed, and the owner of the upper story told the owner of the house (lower story) to (re)build, but he (the lower story owner) did not want to (re) build, the owner of the upper story may (re)build the house** (just the lower story) **and live in it until he** (the owner of the lower story) **reimburses him** (the owner of the upper story) **for his expenses. Rabbi Yehudah said: 'Even so, this individual** (the owner of the upper story) **is living in the other's space** (the rebuilt lower story), **so he must**

pay him rent. Rather, let the owner of the upper story (re)build both the house and the upper story, put the roof on above the upper story (but occupy the ground-floor apartment) until he (the owner of the ground-floor apartment) reimburses him.'

This mishnah requires some explanation. The building discussed is a two-story structure owned by the occupants of the lower and upper floors, each of whom owns the apartment he is living in. The building collapses and is completely destroyed. The second-story owner can only rebuild his apartment after the ground-floor owner has rebuilt the lower part of the building. If the latter refuses to rebuild, what option does the second-story owner have? The mishnah rules that the second-story owner should rebuild the ground-floor apartment and then live in it until the lower-floor owner agrees to reimburse him for the costs incurred in rebuilding the lower floor. When he is reimbursed, the second-story owner can then use this money to rebuild his own dwelling on the second-story. (Alternatively, though the mishnah does not mention this, the second-story owner could rebuild the whole structure at his own expense, live upstairs in his own apartment, but prevent the lower floor owner from occupying the ground floor apartment until he is appropriately reimbursed.)

The second part of the mishnah reveals that Rabbi Yehudah disputes the mishnah's ruling. Since basic Jewish law dictates that a person must pay for any monetary benefit received, Rabbi Yehudah contends that if the upper-floor owner rebuilds the ground floor and lives in it, since he does not own it, he cannot live there rent-free. Not-withstanding the fact that he paid to rebuild the ground floor, the property is not his and he is forbidden to benefit from it without paying rent. In order to prevent this situation from arising, Rabbi Yehudah suggests that the second-story owner rebuild the upper floor too. Once he does this, he can even live on the ground floor rent-free. Logic dictates that since under this scenario the second-story owner could now live in his own apartment rent-free, he derives no monetary benefit from living on the ground floor rent-free. Having removed the possibility of unjustly enriching himself by living on the ground floor rent-free, the second-story owner can now justifiably inhabit the ground floor until its owner reimburses his construction expenses.

Others suggest that Rabbi Yehudah was concerned that by rebuilding the ground floor, the second-story owner has effectively lent its owner money to rebuild his property. By Torah law, lending money with interest is forbidden. Rabbi Yehudah is concerned that after the second-story owner is reimbursed, his living rent-free on the ground floor might actually be – or, might appear to be – interest upon the loan. Therefore, Rabbi Yehudah rules that the second-story owner should not live in the ground-floor apartment unless the second-story apartment has also been rebuilt, so that he incurs no rental fee for living on the ground floor.

The Rabbis question whether Rabbi Yehudah's solution would actually prevent the second-story owner from being unjustly enriched by living on the ground floor. By living there, the second-story owner receives a benefit above and beyond the rent he would pay on the second-story apartment: not having to climb the stairs. While this is an admittedly minor benefit, the Rabbis contend that any unpaid-for benefit, no matter how small, constitutes unjust enrichment.

If the Rabbis contend that no unpaid for benefit is too small to ignore, does the ground-floor owner benefit in any way by having the second-story owner live in his apartment? Perhaps. By living on the ground floor, the owner of the second-story apartment may actually be benefiting the ground-floor owner monetarily because he is preventing the ground-floor apartment from deteriorating due to prolonged neglect. For instance, if the ceiling springs a leak, he will attend to it immediately because he does not want to get wet. If no one was living there, the leak might turn into a torrent before the owner discovered it. Thus, since both owners benefit, no rent need be paid, and the benefit received by the second-story dweller – of not having to climb stairs – is paid for by his living in the apartment.

MISHNAH FOUR: *The Olive Press, the Unstable Tree or Wall, and the Worker's Wages*

Similarly, (in the case where) an olive press is built into (a cavern carved out of a) rock, and a garden is (planted) on top (of the roof of the cavern), and it (the roof of the cavern, partially) caved in (creating a hole between the rooftop garden and the lower level olive press), the owner of the garden may come down and sow below (on the floor of the cavern near the olive press), until he (the olive press owner) repairs (the roof, literally, builds a dome) over his olive press chamber.

If a wall or a tree fell into the public domain and caused damage, he (the owner of the wall or the tree) is not liable to pay. (But) if they (the authorities) gave him a set time to cut down the tree or take down the wall, and one of them (the wall or the tree) fell within the given time, he (the owner) is not liable. If (one of them fell) after time was up, he is liable.

Someone whose wall was close to his neighbor's garden, and it (the wall) collapsed (into the garden), and he (the garden's owner) said to him (the wall's owner), 'Move your stones,' and he (the wall's owner) replied to him (the garden's owner), 'They (the stones) are yours (to keep for the trouble I caused you, so you move them away),' we do not listen to him (the wall's owner). In a case where he (the garden's owner) accepted (the proposal to clear the stones as payment for taking possession of them), and he (the wall's owner then changed his mind and) **said to him** (the garden's owner), 'Here are your wages (offering cash instead of the stones), **and I will take** (back what is) **mine** (my stones),' **we do not listen to him.**

One who hires a worker to work with him in straw or stubble, and he (the worker) **said to him** (the employer), '**Give me my wages,' and he** (the employer) **replied, 'Take what you did** (the straw you cut for me) **as your wages,' we do not listen to him. In a case where the worker accepts** (the straw), **and he** (the employer changed his mind and) **said to him** (the worker), '**Here is your wage** (in cash) **and I will take** (back what is) **mine** (the straw),' **we do not listen to him.**

Our mishnah deals with four separate cases. The first, similar to the first mishnah of the chapter, involves a father who dug out a cave, set up an olive press in the cave, and planted a garden on the roof. He died, leaving the olive press to one son and the rooftop garden to another. As in the first mishnah of this chapter, the question debated in our mishnah concerns what obligation the owner of the olive press chamber below has to the owner of the roof garden above, if the roof partially caves in.

The second part of the mishnah raises the issue of what responsibility the owner of an unstable wall or tree has when it threatens to fall into a public thoroughfare, either blocking it or potentially injuring passersby. If the owner is warned by the authorities to remove the unstable structure, what is his liability if it falls? The mishnah rules that once warned, the owner has thirty days to cut down the tree or destroy the wall. If he fails to do so within the allotted time frame and it falls, he is liable for any damage it causes.

If the wall was poorly constructed to begin with, or is likely to fall before the thirty-day grace period is up, the owner may be liable from the time he is warned. Moreover, he cannot abdicate his responsibility by declaring the wall or tree ownerless before it falls because he has been warned of the impending danger.

The third part of the mishnah involves a wall that collapsed, spilling stones into a neighbor's yard. The owner of the yard asks the owner of the wall to remove his stones. The owner of the stones suggests that the yard's owner clear them for him, keeping the stones as payment for this service. If the owner of the yard agrees, the stones may serve as payment; however, if he does not agree, the owner of the stones is obligated to pay for their removal. If the owner of the yard exercises his right to keep his property clean and removes them himself, the stones' owner is obligated to pay him for this service.

The fourth part of the mishnah deals with the salary due a worker who helps clear a field of straw or other growth: can he be paid in growth of the field rather than in cash? The mishnah quite clearly rules that this can only be done with the worker's consent. By Torah law, the rights of the worker are protected by the commandment to pay the worker on the day he has worked. The employer must not delay paying him. Given this restriction, the employer may be tempted to use whatever of value he has on hand to pay with. The Rabbis have explained that if the worker is paid in goods, he will have to go to the trouble of selling them in order to get cash, and, in addition to the loss of time necessary to find a buyer, he may be forced to pay a conversion fee in selling the goods, thus, losing some of his rightful pay. Nevertheless, the Rabbis add that it may be possible to force the worker to accept foodstuffs (for instance, wheat or barley) in lieu of cash because the worker can either make use of the food as is, or can readily convert the food into cash at current market value. Some Rabbis argue that only ready-to-eat foods, such as bread, may be forced on the employee in payment; thus, wheat and barley, as they must be processed before being eaten, could not be used.

MISHNAH FIVE: *Placing or Storing Privately Owned Objects in the Public Domain*

(In the case where) **one places manure in the public domain, the placer places, and the fertilizer fertilizes** (immediately after the manure has been placed in the public domain, so no obstruction is created). **One may not soak clay in the public domain** (for the purpose of making bricks) **nor may one make bricks** (in the public domain, as the drying of the bricks obstructs the public domain for a long time). **However, one may knead clay in the public domain, if it is not for making bricks** (as just preparing the clay for mortar creates an obstruction for only a brief time). (In a case where) **one builds in the public domain, the stone bringer brings, and the builder builds** (using the stones immediately). **But if he** (the builder) **caused damage** (because he stored materials in the public domain), **he pays for the damage caused. Rabban Shimon ben Gamliel maintains: The builder may even begin setting up his building materials** (up to) **thirty days** (before).

The mishnah describes a number of privately owned objects that may be left or stored in the public domain for their owner's benefit, even though they may cause damage to others who are legitimately using the public domain. The mishnah legislates which types of privately owned objects may be stored in the public domain, and who is liable if they cause damage. The mishnah cites three examples: manure, which is placed in the public domain so that someone else can haul it away to use as fertilizer; clay, which can be conveniently worked upon in the public domain in order to be turned into mortar (but not brick); and stones, which the builder can store in a public staging area close to a building site in the private domain. The mishnah rules that placing manure or leaving clay (to produce mortar) in the public domain is permissible, but leaving clay to soak or to be kneaded for the purpose of forming bricks is not. Apparently, objects that will be left in the public domain for only a short period of time, such as manure, which will quickly be removed to be used as fertilizer, or clay that will quickly be removed to be used as mortar, may be left. However, objects that may be present for a longer period of time, such as clay that needs to be worked into brick, may not be left. Following this logic, the mishnah states that you may only store building bricks in the public domain if you intend to use them immediately. Rabban Shimon ben Gamliel argues in favor of a longer storage period. However, ultimately, the mishnah rules that if an article you left or stored in the public domain damages another, you are liable.

MISHNAH SIX: *Whose Garden Is It?*

(In the case where) **there are two gardens** (each owned by a different person), **one above the other, and vegetables** (grow out of the cliffside) **between them** (on the vertical drop between the two gardens, **Rabbi Meir rules: 'They** (the vegetables) **belong to the upper** (garden).' **Rabbi Yehudah rules: 'They** (the vegetables) **belong to the lower** (garden).' **Argued Rabbi Meir: 'If the** (owner of the) **upper** (garden) **wants to remove his dirt** (down to the level of the lower garden), **there would be no vegetables** (growing on the cliffside; indeed, there would be no cliff).' **Responded Rabbi Yehudah: 'If the**

(owner of the) lower (garden) wanted to fill his garden up (with soil) **there would be no vegetables** (growing on the cliffside; indeed, there would be no cliff). **Then, Rabbi Meir said: 'Since each of them can protest the other's ownership, we establish where the vegetables get their nourishment from.' Rabbi Shimon declared: 'Whatever the** (owner of the) **upper** (garden) **can reach and pick by stretching out his hand belongs to him, and the rest belongs to the** (owner of the) **lower (garden).'**

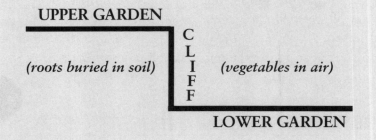

The mishnah presents us with a situation where there is a vertical drop stretching between two gardens: one garden located at the top of a cliff and the other at its base. Vegetables grow horizontally out of the side of the cliff between them. Who owns this produce? Since the soil clearly belongs to the upper garden, do the vegetables belong to the owner of the upper garden? Or since the produce is growing into the airspace above the lower garden do the vegetables belong to the owner of the lower garden? Rabbi Meir argues that the vegetables belong to the owner of the upper garden, as they are rooted in his soil. Supporting this claim, he notes that if the owner of the upper garden chose to remove his soil down to the level of the lower garden, there would be no vegetables to argue over. Rabbi Yehudah argues that owning the roots does not necessarily mean owning the produce, so although he concedes that the roots belong to the owner of the soil (the owner of the upper garden), he argues that the produce growing in the airspace of the lower garden belongs to the lower garden's owner. Supporting this claim, he notes that if the owner of the lower garden chose to add soil to his garden such that it rose to the level of the upper garden, the cliffside would disappear and there would be no vegetables to argue over. As they seem stalemated, Rabbi Meir tries a different approach to support his ruling. He suggests that rather than arguing about which owner can prevent the other from enjoying the produce, why not consider where the produce gets its nourishment from? In his opinion, this would be the roots, the undisputed property of the upper garden's owner.

The Gemara compares several similar situations to see if a principle can be discovered that will resolve this dispute. Rabbi Shimon, perhaps looking ahead to a compromise, suggests that it is possible to find a solution where each shares in some of the produce and yet remains true to the principles of Jewish law. The Gemara will explain how this is possible.

Having reviewed the mishnahs, we are now ready to study their accompanying Gemara.

עין משפט
נר מצוה

מסורת
הש"ס

הבית והעלייה

הבית וְהָעֲלִיָּה בְּרְשׁוּת לְמֹאן קַיְּמָא ט' · וְאִ"ת דְּהֶכָא פְּשִׁיטָא לֵיהּ לְתַלְמִידִי כְּנֶפֶל לְרְשׁוּת דְּחַד מִינַיְיהוּ פָּקֵן מִנֵּיהָא הָוָא שָׁלֵיט נָטֵל כְּלָמֹנוֹס בַּפֶּה וְכָרֵים כְּכָא בַּתְרָא (דף פ"ד) פָּרֵיךְ פְּשִׁיטָא דְּהָם נָפַל הַכּוֹחֵל דְּהַי שֶׁל שְׁנֵיהֶם וּמַטֵּי לָא גְּרִיכָא תְּפַל לְרְשׁוּת חַד וְיֵל מַטֵּי דְּתוּקֵי לֵהּ הָכָא הַמּוּנְחָס כְּגַל זֶה כְּמוֹ כְּגַל זֶה פָּרֵיךְ הַהֵם פְּשִׁיטָא דְּהוּא מְּבַמֵּט לֵיהּ דְּאֹקֵמָיה דּוֹמֶה דְּהֶכָא בִּשְׁנֵיִם לְפָנָיו כְּסָמוּךְ וְעוֹד דְּהֶם (ט) פָּרֵיךְ מַתּוֹךְ הַסָּנָה דְּהַפָּר פָּרֵיךְ פְּשִׁיטָא **לֵימָא** הַיְינוּ הְוַּנְכַּאֵת דְּרַ"לַ הָאֱמַר פָּטוֹר וַאֲבַ"ג דְּמִמַּאֵי דְּרַ"ל

הבית וְהָעֲלִיָּה שֶׁל שְׁנַיִם שֶׁנָּפְלוּ שְׁנֵיהֶם חוֹלְקִין בָּעֵצִים וּבָאֲבָנִים וּבֶעָפָר וְרוֹאִין אֵלּוּ אֲבָנִים הָעֲשׂוּיוֹת לְהִשְׁתַּבֵּר אִם הָיָה אֶחָד מֵהֶן מַכִּיר מִקְצָת אֲבָנָיו נוֹטְלָן וְעוֹלוֹת לוֹ מִן הַחֶשְׁבּוֹן: **גמ'** מֶרְדְּקָנֵי רֹאַן מְכַּלֵּל יְדַאִיכָא לְמוּקָם עֲלַיְהוּ אוֹ בְּחֶבְסָא נָפַל אוֹ בְּחֶבְסָא נָפַל אוֹ הָכִי רֵישָׁא אַבַּאֵי רוֹלְקִין נַחְמוֹ אִי בְּחֶבְסָא נָפַל עֲלַיְתָא אִיתְבוּר אִי צָרִיכָא רַנְפִיל בְּלֵילָא וְלֵיחוֹינְרוּ בְּצָפְרָא דְּפָנֵינָרוּ וְלֵיחֲזוּ מֵאן פָּנֵינָרוּ וְלֵיאֲשֵׁיוֵּיֵּהּ דְּפָנֵינָרוּ בְּגִיר רְשׁוּת הָרַבִּים וְאָזְלוּ לְעָלְבָּא וְלֵיחֲזוּ בְּרִישׁוֹת רְבָּאוְרֹתְבָן וְלֵיחֲזוּ צָרִיךְ הַמְּבַצֵּיא בִּרְכַּיָּי עֲלֵי דְּרָאַיְיה לֹא

הבית וְהָעֲלִיָּה שֶׁל שְׁנַיִם · כֵּיוָן שְׁנֵי אַחִים שֶׁחוֹלְקִין אֶחָד נָטַל בֵּית וְאֶחָד נָטַל עֲלִיָּה שֶׁל הָאֲבָנִים שֶׁל עֲלִיָּה וְלִמְטָה שֶׁל תִּקְרַת הַבַּיִת הַתַּחְתּוֹנָה שֶׁהִיא קַרְקָעִיתָהּ שֶׁל עֲלִיָּה וְגַם שֶׁל תִּקְרַת הַבַּיִת שֶׁל שָׁלוֹן וְהֵימֵנָּה וְלַמְטָה שֶׁל הֶחָזָן : שְׁנֵיהֶם חוֹלְקִים · הַכֹּל לְפִי (א) הַנְּטִיָּה שֶׁהָאֶחָד הָיָה נָטוּי מֵחֲבֵירוֹ וְהָאֲבָנִים וְעָפָר מְרוּבָּה מִשֶּׁל חֲבֵירוֹ חוֹלְקִים לְפִי שֶׁכֵּן נִיכָּר אוֹ אֲבָנִים שֶׁל עֲלִיּוֹן וְאוֹ אֲבָנִים שֶׁל הֶחָזָן : רוֹאִים אֵלּוּ אֲבָנִים רְאוּיוֹת לְהִשָּׁכֵל · אִם יֵשׁ אֲבָנִים שְׁבוּרִיוֹת שֶׁל לְבֵינִים זֶה אוֹמֵר שְׁלֵישׁוֹת שֶׁלִּי רוֹאִין אֵלּוּ אֵם אֲבָנִים רְאוּיוֹת לְהִשָּׁכֵר אֵם שֶׁל עֶלְיוֹן אֵם שֶׁל הֶחָזָן וְהַכֹּל לְפִי הַמַּפֹּלֶת שֶׁאֵם נִתְבַּץ הַבַּיִת מִסִּתְרוֹ וְנָפַל פְּתָחוֹ הַחוֹמָה בִּמְקוֹמָהּ יֵשׁ לִדְפֹק שֶׁהַתַּחְתּוֹעָה נִכְבְּרוּ וְלֹךְ נָפְלָה "הַבַּיִת שֶׁהָיָה שׁוֹמֵד זוֹקֵף וְנָפַל שָׁלֵיוָא שֶׁהָיָה נָכוֹל וְאֹם נָפַל לֹכָן מָמוֹת תַתְבָּו נֵל שְׁכָבִיֵ אָמֵלֹ

תורה אור
(א) רש"י ד"ה מורה
חולקין הכל לפי הנטוה
לפי אם מרובה כ"ה:
נוסח מתיבות : (ב) תוסף
ד"ה ולימא וכו' דהם
מוליכי המכר כנוגל :

Part Two:
THE GEMARA WITH COMMENTARY

MISHNAH ONE: *A House Collapses*

(In this first case) a house **(lower story)** and an upper story belonging to two people collapsed. The two owners split the wood, the stones, and the mortar. And we **(the court)** determine which stones are likely to have broken. If one of them recognizes some of his stones, he takes them, but they count for him as part of his reckoning.

For a brief commentary on this mishnah, see Part One page 16. To a layperson the mishnah seems fairly straightforward and clear; however, the Gemara will now analyze the mishnah showing why a court may be necessary to help the owners split the rubble.

GEMARA

The mishnah, after presenting the basic case, issues four rulings in the following order: (1) The two owners split the rubble proportionally, in accord with their losses; (2) By examining the rubble, the court attempts to determine which material belongs to which owner so that the owners can regain their own building materials; (3) If one of the owners recognizes some material as his and identifies it, he may lay claim to it; and (4) Any material claimed by one of the owners is subtracted from the overall division of the material so that the assets are still divided proportionally. The Gemara omits discussing the first ruling for now, considering its proportional split of all assets to be the theoretical basis of the mishnah, a "fall-back" position, if the other three rulings are not wholly applicable. The Gemara attempts to determine the exact circumstances in which the other three rulings come into play, beginning its discussion by investigating the second ruling: the court's attempt to establish ownership by examining the rubble.

> **Since it (the mishnah) rules 'we determine which stones are likely to have broken,' it follows that it is possible to figure out whether downward pressure caused the house to fall or whether it received a (horizontal) push from above. If so, why does the first part (of the mishnah) declare 'the two owners split?' Let's see. If it was pushed and fell, (when we investigate we will see that) the upper story (stones) are broken. If it fell because of downward pressure, (when we investigate we will see that) the bottom story (stones) are broken.**

Clearly without a teacher to explain it, the Gemara is difficult to understand. What does the Gemara mean by "downward pressure" and a "(horizontal) push?" Why should this distinction be significant? The Gemara teaches us that by examining the rubble it may be possible to determine which stones fell from the upper story and which from the lower one. If the court succeeds at this, then the court can determine who owns which stones and instead of just splitting the rubble using a fixed formula, the court can award the stones to their original owners. The Gemara suggests, for instance, that if the building collapsed because the foundation caved in due to downward pressure, then the broken stones at the bottom of the pile will be from the ground floor, while the whole stones at the top of pile will be from the second floor. In such a case, the owner of the upper floor will be awarded the whole stones. If the building was toppled by the wind, then it is more likely that the upper floor's stones broke, as these stones fell farther and from a greater height. Additionally, the upper floor's stones will not be sitting on top of the intact foundation stones; rather, they will have been blown a certain distance away by the wind. In such a case, the owner of the ground floor would be awarded the whole stones. Therefore when the mishnah rules that the partners split the material proportionally, it really means they only split the material this way when each owner's rubble cannot be determined.

However, perhaps in some cases the court will be unable to make the necessary determination of ownership by direct inspection of the rubble. The Gemara will now suggest that other factors may be brought into play to aid us in deciding how to divide the material between the two owners.

It (the ruling of splitting the assets proportionally) **is not necessary unless** (the wall) **fell at night** (because then no one saw how the stones were scattered). **But** (even in such a case) **let us look** (at the distribution of the stones) **in the morning. But they** (the stones, in this hypothetical case) **were removed already** (by passersby). **So let us see who took them away and ask them.** (It is a case where) **people in the street removed them and left. But let us see whose property they** (the stones) **are in so that the other party will have to bring proof. But if the stones are in a courtyard belonging to both parties, or in a public domain, or if you prefer, in a situation where the partners are not particular about each other's property** (than where the stones lie is no proof of ownership).

We learned above that we might be able to tell who owns the whole stones by studying the way they were scattered on the ground. But suppose they fell at night, when no one was around to witness the collapse of the building. Would the scatter pattern of broken and whole stones we see in the morning still be evidence of who owned the whole stones? Perhaps, if the stones lay untouched until daylight. But suppose that they had been moved by townspeople or passersby who wanted to clear the rubble from the public thoroughfare. That would make direct inspection of the scatter pattern unreliable for determining ownership. If the people who cleared the stones from the roadway were still available, we could ask them what the original pattern was. But, having cleared the public thoroughfare of the stones, they likely have gone their separate ways and are unavailable to testify. We are left with a pile of stones whose pattern now teaches us nothing about who owns them. If such a pile rests in the public domain, or on property jointly owned by both apartment owners, than perhaps this is the case mentioned in the mishnah where the court splits the stones proportionally without attempting to determine who the stones originally belonged to.

But suppose when the stones were cleared away, they were placed in a pile on property belonging to only one of the apartment owners. Then a fundamental principle of Talmudic law could be employed to determine ownership: objects with no identified owner can be claimed by any individual in whose private domain they are resting. If an individual's private property belongs exclusively to him, an object's presence in it allows him to lay claim to it. In our case this would create a problem for the owner of the other apartment, as he would need to bring proof that some of the stones belong to him. Absent that proof, he would be unable to demand that the court remove them from the other's possession. Removal of material from a person's possession invokes a different, fundamental maxim of Talmudic law: we do not remove money or other property from someone's possession without the claimant presenting proof of his claim. (See *Bava Kamma* 46b where the Gemara rules that the burden of proof rests upon the one seeking to remove property from the possession of another.)

The Gemara suggests that even in this situation we can continue to advance the principle of proportional division of assets if the owners do not view their properties as exclusive. That is to say, being partners or brothers, each one has freely placed his own possessions in the other's private domain in the past. Therefore, since in the past the owners were not particular about using each other's space, the stones' presence in one of their properties cannot now be used to support an ownership claim. If investigations such as this continue to result in no clear determination of ownership over some or over all of the assets then the court applies the first ruling of the mishnah and splits all the assets proportionally.

This is as far as the Gemara goes in teaching us how to determine ownership by observing the pattern of debris. The discussion is neither exhaustive nor comprehensive; however, it fulfills its goal of providing us with some basics for determining ownership. The Gemara now turns its attention to the third ruling of the mishnah: one of the owner's recognizing his own building material. Suppose in the pile of rubble one of the owners is sure he recognizes whole stones that came from his apartment. Can he claim them? The mishnah rules that such recognition can provide him with a valid claim. The Gemara will now qualify the limits of that claim.

'If one of them (one of the apartment owners) **recognizes** (some of his stones),' **what does the other** (apartment owner) **claim? If he says 'yes,' it is obvious. And if he does not say 'yes,' why does he** (the claimant) **take** (the stones he recognizes since both owners seems to have equal claims)? **Rather,** (the case the mishnah discusses must be when) **he responds: 'I do not know.'**

One owner claims he recognizes some of his stones, presumably whole ones, as they are the most recognizable and the most valuable for rebuilding. If the second owner assents, the stones' ownership is no longer in question. That is why the Gemara says, "If he says 'yes,' it is obvious." If the second owner protests that he actually owns these same exact stones, the first claimant cannot take the stones, as the two potential owners have made equally impassioned claims with no evidence to back them up. This is the legal impasse the Gemara is referring to when it says, "And if he does not say 'yes,' why does he take?" In this instance, the mishnah's first ruling, namely, splitting the assets proportionally comes back into play.

The Gemara, therefore, chooses to explain that the mishnah is discussing a third case, one where the second owner admits he is unsure whom the stones belong to: "Rather, he responds: 'I do not know.' "Does the respondent's uncertainty manage to nullify the other owner's claim, or does it support it? The Talmud resolves the matter in consonance with the mishnah's ruling of "take them," by employing the principle of "certainty versus doubt": a claim made with "certainty" is considered stronger than a claim made based upon "doubt," and so it will usually win out. (This does not apply to a case where there is other solid evidence proving ownership, as above.) The case the Gemara has posited seems to be such a case. The Gemara now cites several cases, discussed elsewhere in the Talmud, concerning claims of certainty versus doubt, to help us learn whether and how this principle is applicable in our case.

Let us say that our mishnah is a refutation of Rav Nachman. For we have learned (in the discussion of a case where one person says that) **a *maneh* of mine is in your hand** (a maneh was a monetary unit in Talmudic times) **and the other replies: 'I do not know,' Rav Huna and Rav Yehudah rule that he is liable, but Rav Nachman and Rabbi Yochanan rule he is exempt** (from paying).

Elsewhere in the Talmud, the Gemara discusses a case where one man says to another, "You owe me some money." The latter replies, "I am not sure that I owe you the money you claim." Neither man has any proof of ownership. Rav Huna and Rav Yehudah rule that since the latter is not sure whether he owes the money or not, but the claimant is sure, the claimant should be paid. Here, the principle of "certainty versus doubt" dictates that the individual who is certain has a stronger case. Rav Nachman and Rabbi Yochanan rule against paying the claimant because the principle that "the burden of proof rests upon the one seeking to extract property from the possession of another" overrules the principle of "certainty versus doubt."

As applied to our current case (where one says that "These are my stones," and the other says that "I am not sure"), Rav Huna and Rav Yehudah would rule that since certainty trumps doubt, the claimant should keep the stones he recognizes, despite the other's doubts. Rav Nachman and Rabbi Yochanan would rule that the respondent's doubt is strong enough to prevent the claimant from taking possession of the stones, absent definitive proof, for "the burden of proof rests upon the one seeking to extract property from another."

Since the mishnah – assuming that it is discussing the case of certainty and doubt, as the Gemara now does – possesses an authoritative voice in this argument, and has, thus, ruled that recognition can lead to ownership, the Gemara begins its discussion of the case from elsewhere in the Talmud by asking, "Shall we say our mishnah is a refutation of Rav Nachman?" because Rav Nachman, based upon his ruling in the comparison case, would seem to refute the notion that recognition alone can determine ownership.

Even after comparing the cases, the Gemara is reluctant to rule against Rav Nachman; therefore, it searches for another case to compare to the mishnah, hoping that a guiding principle will be found to resolve the apparent dispute between our mishnah and Rav Nachman. Since this new case also involves Rav Nachman, perhaps we can now reach an understanding of our mishnah that does not contradict his opinions in either case. Here is the second case:

> **Rav Nachman said elsewhere: 'For example, where there is a business** (transaction) **involving an oath between them.' Here too** (in our mishnah, regarding the discussion of whose stones they are, the case also concerns) **a business** (transaction) **involving an oath. As Rava said, for Rava said that** (the case is one where one person says) **'A maneh of mine is in your hand,' and the other replies, 'Only half of that which** (you claim) **is yours is in my hand, and I do not know if I owe you the rest.' Since he cannot swear** (regarding who owns the remaining half) **he must** (turn over the part he does not dispute, and) **pay** (the balance he questions owing, but cannot swear to).

In this second case, Rav Nachman rules that in certain circumstances the court can obligate an individual who partially admits his debt to take an oath. For instance, in a case where one man claims another owes him money, and the other admits that he owes some, but definitely not all, of the money claimed. In the classical formulation of this case where the defendant admits he owes the claimant half of his claim, but denies owing any more, the court can force the defendant to take an oath establishing his veracity vis-à-vis the second half. Complicating the matter, if in this case the defendant is unsure of whether or not he owes the second half, since he is unable to swear with absolute certainty one way or another, he must pay the claimant in full.

Remember that taking an oath means invoking God as your witness, a matter not to be taken lightly. Most courts will advise defendants that even when they have no doubt about their claim and feel comfortable taking an oath, that it is preferable to forgo the oath and lose the money, rather than risk unintentionally desecrating God's name. For how often have we been quite certain of the truth, only to discover later that our memory was faulty, or that we did not have a clear understanding of the entire picture. We certainly had no intention to lie, but still, as events later revealed, we did not speak the truth. One need not be lying to shy away from an oath. An oath is sworn before a court; the Torah is ceremonially taken out of the ark and the witness holds it in his arms while he swears. The Rabbis teach us that the Heavens shake when an oath – true or false – is uttered. Therefore, the Rabbis would rather the defendant pay money he believes he does not owe than take an oath. In our case, in the Gemara, how can anyone be absolutely sure which stones belong to him. After all, most stones look alike, and even the markings on them may be similar. It is easy for the defendant to be sure and yet wrong about his ownership. Better to cede the stones to the building's other owner than risk a false oath. Applying Rav Nachman's case law to our dispute with the stones, if one party admits that some of the stones claimed belong to his neighbor, but he is unsure about the ownership of all of the stones claimed, he has partially accepted the claimant's contention. According to Rav Nachman, a partial admission places him under an obligation either to swear regarding the disputed part of the claim or to cede it to the claimant. Since the defendant cannot invoke God's name in an oath without being absolutely certain, he forfeits the disputed stones to the claimant when he is unsure who owns them.

Does this resolve the apparent contradiction between the mishnah and Rav Nachman? The mishnah issued the general ruling that by recognizing his stones, the owner could make a valid claim upon them. Rav Nachman believes that recognition can only support a claim of ownership in certain cases. In his opinion, recognition leads to possession only when the defendant agreed to part of the claim, but was unsure about the rest. Since the defendant would be unable to swear regarding the disputed stones, the claimant would receive all of them. However, if the defendant was uncertain about the entire claim, recognition would not necessarily validate ownership. Therefore, to banish the specter of disagreement between Rav Nachman and the mishnah, the Gemara posits that the mishnah is dealing with the case where the defendant admits part of the claim and is unsure about the rest. Here, then, is a summary of what we have learned concerning the mishnah's statement that recognition leads to ownership:

- If one owner claims to recognize certain stones as his, and the other does not disagree, recognition leads to ownership.

- If one owner claims to recognize certain stones as his, but the other claims they are his, the court divides the assets proportionally (applying the first ruling of the mishnah).

- If one partner claims to recognize certain stones as his, and the other is uncertain, we are less sure about how to resolve the dispute. The principle of "certainty versus doubt" may force the court to rule that certainty carries the day, and the claimant keeps the material that he recognized as his own.

- If one owner claims to recognize certain stones as his, and the other agrees regarding some stones, but is uncertain regarding others, the latter must either take an oath regarding his ownership of the disputed stones, or he must forfeit them.

This is as close as we can come to reconciling the various opinions concerning the mishnah's ruling in the case of recognition. We can go no farther, and the Talmud refuses to provide any more resolutions of the counterclaims. We now move on to the final point the mishnah dealt with: how to divide the remaining building material once someone has taken the part of the rubble he recognized.

'But they (the stones he recognized and acquired) **count for him as part of his reckoning.' Rava thought to say according to the reckoning of the broken ones** (stones). **Thus, since the defendant said, 'I don't know,' he** (his case) **is weaker. Abaye said to him** (Rava): **'Surely the opposite is true: the other one** (who recognized his whole stones) **is** (in a) **weaker** (position) **since he identified these**

(stones) **and not any others; thus, he does not own any others; all the other** (whole stones) **belong to the other party.' Rather, continued Abaye, '(it must mean) that** (they count only) **towards his total of whole stones.' If so, how did he** (the one who identified his stones) **benefit** (from his identification)? **Where** (the stones) **were wider** (and so of more value) **or the clay** (of which the stones were made) **was of good quality.**

An argument ensues between Rava and Abaye regarding how the stones are to be divided once recognition awards one partner a certain number of whole stones. For instance, in a case where there were one hundred whole stones and one hundred broken ones, if one owner identifies twenty whole stones as his own and is awarded them by the court, how are the remaining whole stones divided? Perhaps, the eighty remaining whole stones are divided equally, forty going to each owner. If so, one owner will wind up with twenty plus forty, or sixty whole stones, while the other will receive only forty whole stones. Given that the building materials must ultimately be split proportionally (for the moment, lets assume the apartments were the same size, so the proportional split would be fifty-fifty), then the first owner would receive sixty whole stones and forty broken ones, while the second would receive forty whole stones and sixty broken ones. This division of assets is suggested by Rava in the Gemara. Abaye has a different view. He suggests that by identifying twenty whole stones as his own, the first owner has tacitly admitted that he cannot identify the other eighty whole stones as his own, and, therefore, the other owner should be entitled to them. If so under the rule of proportionality, the first owner would be awarded twenty whole stones and eighty broken ones, while the second would receive the eighty unidentified, whole stones and twenty broken ones. According to Abaye, the one who recognizes some of his stones seems penalized for his recognition. Realizing this, the Gemara asks, "If so, how did he (the one who identified his stones) benefit?"

We might answer that the mishnah demands a proportional split, so perhaps we need to ensure that each owner gets his proportional split of the whole stones. Therefore, the identified stones must be included in the reckoning of whole stones the owner receives. For instance, if he receives fifty out of one hundred whole stones, twenty of these are the stones he identified. Thus, each owner would be awarded fifty whole and fifty broken stones, but some of the whole stones the first owner received would be stones he recognized. However, if this solution is correct, we still must answer the Gemara's question – "How did he benefit (by identifying the stones)?" – for the final division will be the same.

The Talmud adopts this solution and suggests an advantage: the particular stones he identified are higher-quality ones as they did not break and, therefore, are better to rebuild with. Left unsaid by the Gemara, although of pre-eminent importance, is that such a division brings strict equality to the process, a goal to be mightily striven for in resolving any business situation with conflicting interests.

Although the Gemara expends much effort discussing methods of resolving the conflict between the owners, note that the mishnah's first ruling was to split all the material proportionally. The default ruling, if the true owner's identity cannot be discovered by observing the scatter pattern of the debris, or by one of the owners identifying his own stones, is to split the material proportionally. Given this, it would have made sense for the mishnah to cite this ruling last. However, the Talmud orders its rulings with great care. It clearly cited this ruling first for a reason. Perhaps the commentators' suggestion that these two owners may be brothers, and the house an inheritance from their father, offers the key to understanding the mishnah's order. Perhaps the mishnah, by first suggesting that the disputants split the assets proportionally, is asking these two brothers (or partners) to forgo the legal technicalities and choose the proportional division of assets. It is hard to imagine that their father had such court cases in mind when he left them the inheritance to share. He just wanted each of them to have a place to live. Any conflict would then be a dishonor to his memory. If the disputants are partners, this logic can also apply for we expect partners, who are after all fellow Israelites, to act as charitably as brothers.

Ethical Insights: Sanctifying the Mundane

In the Introduction, I mentioned that by regulating business transactions the Torah both minimizes conflict and, more importantly, introduces holiness into the everyday working world. As I concluded above, while there are legal avenues available to ensure a fair division of assets, perhaps brothers, or partners, should go beyond the letter of the law when resolving monetary conflicts. In Tractate *Bava Kamma* 27a–27b, the Rabbis address another common business interaction and provide guidelines for sanctifying it.

MISHNAH

If one places a jug in the public domain and another (person) came and tripped on it (the jug) and broke it, he (the person who tripped) is not liable (for damage caused to the jug). And if he (the person who tripped) was injured by it (the jug, itself, or by his tripping over the jug), the owner of the barrel is liable for the damage caused (the damage done to the one who tripped).

Everyone has the right to use public space such as the street, the market, or a public square. People have the legal right to traverse the public domain to carry out their daily tasks; therefore, everyone is even allowed to carry goods in the public domain. However, with this right comes responsibility, especially since the use of public space is rarely conflict-free. If one individual causes injury or damage to another, this responsibility translates into liability which usually has a dollar figure attached.

Our mishnah delineates and rules upon some of these conflicts. If an individual set his jug down in the public domain for a moment, perhaps to take a rest from his burden or perhaps to do some quick shopping in a nearby store, and another person accidentally tripped over the vessel and broke it, the one who tripped is not responsible for damaging the vessel or ruining its contents since the owner of the vessel has no more right to set it down in the public domain than the tripper has to walk there. Moreover, if the one who tripped was injured by his fall or by the jug's broken fragments, the jug's owner is liable. Likewise, if someone else walked by and the vessel's contents or its jagged fragments caused him injury or damage (he slipped on the spillage or was cut by the fragments; his clothes were stained or torn), the broken vessel's owner is liable, not the one who broke the vessel.

The Gemara begins investigating this mishnah by focusing upon a different issue than we might have expected. Rather than analyzing issues surrounding liability for damages, it focuses upon defining the vessel under discussion. It does so because, as we shall see, a crucial principle of business practice, and a strong moral lesson, is taught by the mishnah's choice of vessel.

GEMARA

He opens with a jug and ends with a barrel. And we have also learned in another mishnah (later in the same talmudic chapter): **'If this one comes with his barrel and that one comes with his beam and the jug of this one was broken by the beam of that one, he** (the owner of the beam) **is exempt from liability.'** (Here) **he** (the narrator)

begins (the discussion) **with a barrel and ends with a jug** (interchanging the names of the broken vessel). **And we have also learned in another mishnah** (later in the same chapter): **'This one came with his barrel of wine and that one came with his jug of honey. The barrel of honey split open and** (the owner of the barrel of wine) **spilled out his wine and saved the honey** (by filling his empty barrel with what was left of the barrel of honey), **he gets only his wages** (for the work he did, but no payment for the lost wine).' Here again, he (the narrator) **opens with a jug and ends with a barrel. Rav Papa said: 'Jug and barrel are the same.' So why differentiate? For buying and selling. What is the case** (or locale, where this differentiation matters)? **If we say** (we are referring to) **a place where a jug is not referred to as a barrel and a barrel is not referred to as a jug,** in a case where one is not referred to by the name of the other, we do not need to discuss the issue. **No, it is needed for a place where most people refer to a barrel as a barrel and most refer to a jug as a jug, but there are also those** (albeit a minority) **who call a jug a barrel and a barrel a jug. You might have thought that we** (the law) **follow** (what) **most people** (do). **This teaches us that we do not follow the majority in money matters.**

Again, it would seem appropriate for the Gemara to begin its discussion of the mishnah by exploring the issues surrounding its central theme: liability incurred by someone leaving his or her vessel in the public domain. However, this is not how the Rabbis choose to begin their discussion. Instead, the Gemara digresses, focusing upon a seemingly irrelevant detail in the mishnah, that of the mishnah opening by referring to the broken vessel as a *chavit*, literally a barrel, and thereafter referring to it as a *kad*, literally a jug. Thus, the Gemara opens its discussion with the phrase, "He begins with a jug and ends with a barrel." Since a barrel is presumably far larger than a jug, the Gemara asks how these two terms can be used interchangeably.

Strengthening its question, the Gemara then cites two other cases where the author of the Mishnah used the terms interchangeably, thus confirming that the anomaly in our mishnah is not simply an error of transmission. Both examples are introduced by the phrase, "And we have also learned in another mishnah." The first example introduces a man with a beam accidentally striking another man's barrel in the public domain. The broken vessel is at first referred to as a barrel and later referred to as a jug. The second example involves two men: one with a barrel that contains honey, and another with a vessel containing wine. Wine being cheaper than honey, when the jug filled with honey spontaneously develops a crack, the owner of the wine spills his wine on the ground so that he can use his empty vessel to save the other's honey. The mishnah rules that the wine's owner, acting on his own volition to save the honey, cannot expect any reimbursement for his lost wine, but must be paid as a hired worker would have been paid for helping to transfer the honey (and, presumably, receives a thank-you from the grateful owner of the honey). The Gemara ignores the fairness of this repayment, focusing again on the mishnah's seemingly random use of the terms barrel and jug for the honey vessel.

As legalists, presumably the Rabbis would want to use the difficulty in these mishnahs to define the difference between a barrel and a jug so as to minimize conflict and misunderstanding between buyers and sellers. However, instead the Rabbis use these mishnahs to teach that not even common usage necessarily distinguishes between the two vessels, for in some places a minority of people use the terms interchangeably. The Rabbis teach us that in money matters, the two people involved in a transaction must clearly understand each other's intentions. Neither must fool the other by using ambiguous wording. Each must accept responsibility for knowing what he is contracting to buy or sell.

In tractate *Bava Metzia* 48a, the Talmud establishes that in order to prevent misunderstandings no transaction involving movable goods may be finalized without the buyer taking physical possession of the object. Even if money has changed hands, title to the object has not, and the buyer may back out (the seller, having received money, may not). For instance, if a person paid money for what he thought was a barrel, but discovered later that he had only paid for a jug, he could back out of the deal and have his money returned if he had not yet taken possession of the vessel. This notwithstanding, the Rabbis emphasize that each party must honor its promises. A monetary payment, although not binding, indicates that both the buyer and the seller have reached an agreement. Even though the buyer may retract at this point, the Rabbis record the following curse to be visited upon anyone who retracts after verbally agreeing to a deal:

The Sages said: 'The One Who took retribution from the people of the Generation of the Flood and the people of the Generation of the Dispersion and from the people of Sodom and Gomorrah and from the Egyptians at the Sea [of Reeds] will in the future take retribution from someone who does not stand by his words... although one who buys and sells with words has not acquired anything, the spirit of the Sages is not comfortable with what he has done.'

Perhaps the Sages refuse to define how small a barrel is and how large a jug may be so that both sides are forced to verify exactly what is being bought or sold before reaching an agreement. Having verified the matter carefully, they are less likely to renege on their promises.

The Rabbis of the Talmud also harshly condemn a seller who attempts to verbally defraud another by selling him, for example, a jug's worth of wine after leading him to believe – or after being aware that he expects to receive – a barrel's worth, or vice versa. The Rabbis apply the following verse to behavior of this sort: "And if you sell anything to your neighbor or buy anything from him, you shall not wrong one another… but you shall fear your God (*Leviticus* 25:14–17)." The Rabbis stress the end of the verse: "you shall fear your God." The Torah emphasizes the need to place fear of God front and center when performing a business transaction so that honesty is maintained both in word and in deed. The Talmud, in Tractate *Bava Metzia* 58b, notes that regarding "any matter that is known only to the heart [which is hidden from other human beings], it is stated: 'You shall fear your God.'" God, who can see into human hearts, will hold a seller who implied a barrel's worth, but sold a jug's worth, accountable for his sin.

God is present during the course of every human interaction. Even the most mundane business or personal dealings present opportunities for infusing the world with holiness or sullying it with sin. It is in the everyday world that our morality is most tested and our behavior most judged. Tractate *Bava Metzia*, falling as it does in the order of *Damages*, dealing with civil law, is where many of these issues are debated. Therefore, the study of such mundane issues as building codes, partnership agreements, landlord and tenant relationships, and the like, found in our chapter of Talmud, is an excellent entree into the talmudic way of thinking and of evaluating right actions. As the Sages declare in Tractate *Bava Kamma* 30a, "Any person who wants to be righteous [must study and] obey the laws of damages (such as those found in our current chapter)."

MISHNAH TWO: *A Hole in the Floor*

(In the case of) **a house** (ground floor) **with an upper story** (second floor), **the upper story's** (floor partially) **caved in** (creating an open hole between the two dwellings), **and the owner of the building** (who lives on the ground floor) **does not want to fix it. The occupant of the upper story** (a renter) **may descend and live downstairs until he** (the building's owner) **repairs the second story's floor. Rabbi Yose says that the** (building's owner, living on the) **lower** (floor) **provides** (the material for the part of) **the ceiling** (that acts as a foundation for repairing the hole in the upstairs floor) **and the˙upper** (floor occupant, the renter) **provides the plaster** (to cover the foundation provided by the owner).

For a brief commentary on this mishnah, see Part One page 17.

GEMARA

How big must the opening be? Rav says: 'Most (of the floor).' **Shmuel says: 'Four** (handbreadths). **Rav rules most** (of the floor), **but if four handbreadths, no, because a person can live part** (of the time) **below and part** (of the time) **above. Shmuel rules only four handbreadths, because a person cannot live part below and part above.**

"How big must the opening be" refers to how much floor must collapse before, as the mishnah rules, the upper-floor tenant can move into the lower apartment with the landlord. Rav and Shmuel disagree as to how much of the floor must collapse before the court obligates an apartment-sharing arrangement. Rav says most of the floor must collapse before the tenant can move downstairs. Shmuel says only four handbreadths need collapse before the tenant can move downstairs. Rav counters that if only four handbreadths have collapsed, the tenant could quite reasonably be granted an equivalent space in the owner's downstairs apartment to make up for any loss of floor space he has suffered; moving completely into the landlord's apartment is hardly necessary. According to Rav, if the tenant had kept a flowerpot in that small collapsed area, the landlord could be forced to store it in his apartment where the tenant could come down to feed it when necessary. This ruling forces the tenant to "live" in two places at the same time, but Rav feels that this is a reasonable request to make. Shmuel argues that even a collapse as small as four handbreadths makes the upper dwelling uninhabitable, since the tenant cannot reasonably be expected to live in two places at the same time. According to Shmuel, the landlord must share his entire apartment with the tenant until the ceiling/floor is fixed, even if only four handbreadths have collapsed.

Note that monetary compensation, such as rent abatement, is not raised as an option. Additionally, neither safety issues nor privacy rights are discussed here. Although these issues may be relevant, they are addressed elsewhere in the Talmud. Most crucially, the Gemara fails to either resolve or rule upon the dispute between Rav and Shmuel at this time. Instead, the Gemara abandons the above approach, choosing instead to explore the type of contract the landlord and tenant had. Perhaps that avenue of investigation will prove a better one to determining where responsibility lies.

What are the circumstances (in the mishnah)? **If** (the landlord) **said** (to the tenant), '(I am renting) *this* **upper apartment** (to you),' (the apartment) **has gone** (and that ends the obligation). **Rather, where he** (the landlord) **said, 'An upper apartment** (without specifying a particular apartment).' **Let him** (the landlord) **rent another** (upper apartment) **to him** (the tenant). **Rava said: 'No,** (the ruling of the mishnah) **applies to the case where he** (the landlord) **said: 'This upper apartment, which I am renting to you, when it goes up, go up with it, and when it goes down, go down with it** (that is, when it collapses, move down to my place).' **But if so, why** (does the mishnah) **mention** (the case at all)? **Rav Ashi said: 'Where he** (the landlord) **said: "This upper apartment which is on top of this lower apartment I am renting to you," because then he pledges the house** (lower apartment in support of) **the upper apartment.' Ravin bar Rav Adda related a similar case in the name of Rabbi Yitzchak: 'An incident, concerning one person who said to another: "This vine which is on top of the peach tree, I am selling to you." The peach tree was subsequently uprooted. The case came before Rabbi Chiya, and he ruled: "You are obligated to put up a peach tree for him as long as the vine exists." '**

The Gemara illustrates that the language used in the original oral agreement (the verbal contract) is crucial to resolving when the tenant may move in with the landlord. This is what the Gemara means when it asks: "What are the circumstances?" That is to say, what language was used in the rental agreement? For example, if the landlord specified in the original verbal contract that only this particular upper apartment was being rented, if the apartment is destroyed or rendered uninhabitable, the contract is void, and the tenant has no claim upon the landlord ("I am renting *this* apartment to you"). If the landlord did specify that he was renting an upper apartment, but did not specify which one, then if the apartment becomes uninhabitable, he is obligated to provide the tenant with any other upper apartment to fulfill the terms of the agreement ("Let him rent another to him").

So in which case is the ruling of the mishnah (that the lower apartment must be shared) applicable? Perhaps, Rav Ashi answers, when the tenant insisted on an addition to the contract, in which the landlord provided his lower apartment as part of a guarantee that the tenant would always have an apartment to live in at that location, even if the upper apartment he was renting became uninhabitable. The Gemara agrees that this could be the mishnah's case; however, since the contract itself specifies the circumstances under which the tenant may move downstairs, there would be no need for our mishnah to rule on this case. It is an open and shut case. So this is not the case of the mishnah.

The Gemara suggests another case in which the guarantee given pledging the lower apartment in support of the upper one is weaker; thus, demonstrating the need for our mishnah's ruling. The Gemara then cites Ravin's story about the peach tree and the vine, to demonstrate how powerful the force of a guarantee can be. One man sold another a vine on top of a peach tree. Only the vine was sold, not the peach tree. The tree remained in its original owner's hands; however, the vine's survival was predicated on the existence of the peach tree. When the peach tree was destroyed, the vine had no supporting structure. Rabbi Chiya's court ruled that the peach tree's owner must replace the tree, in order to continue to support the vine. Thus, by analogy, there is no limit to the upper-floor tenant's right to a place to live as long as the lower apartment pledged to support the rental of the upper apartment exists. This is the case the mishnah speaks of.

Having proven that at least under certain contractual conditions, the right of the tenant to move into the landlord's ground-floor apartment is unchallengeable, the Gemara now attempts to define the scope of that right.

Rabbi Abba bar Mamal asked: 'Does he (the tenant) **live alone as before, or perhaps both of them live** (downstairs together), **for he** (the landlord) **can reason with him** (the tenant) **saying, "I did not rent to you with the intention**

of being evicted"?' **If you wish to say that both of them live there** (together), **when he** (the tenant) **uses** (the lower apartment) **does he use it by way of the** (ground-floor) **door or does he use it by way of the ceiling** (entering his own apartment via the upper floor entrance, and then descending to the lower floor apartment through the hole in his floor). **Do we say it must be as at first, just as at first** (he entered) **by way of the roof** (second-story entrance) **so too now by way of the roof? Or perhaps, the** (the tenant) **says to him** (the landlord): **'I agreed to make an ascent** (to the original apartment) **but not to make an ascent and a descent.' If you accept the tenant's assertion, what if the building had two upper floors** (to rent)? **If the uppermost floor caved** (into the second story), **the tenant** (from the third story) **goes down to live on the second floor** (with the second-story tenant). **If the second-story apartment's floor caved in, does the tenant go up to the third floor** (or down to the ground floor with the landlord)? **Do we say that the landlord can reason with the tenant that he accepted a state of ascent upon himself** (and, therefore, must ascend to the third floor as he did to the second floor)? **Or, can the tenant, perhaps, argue that he accepted only one ascent upon himself** (in the rental agreement)? **Let these** (questions) **stand unanswered.**

The Talmud raises a number of questions concerning the scope of the tenant's rights upon moving into his landlord's apartment. Is he permitted to insist that since the landlord's apartment is only a single-family dwelling and he was forced to move out of a single-family dwelling, he cannot be forced to share such a small space and therefore the landlord and his family must move out? Can the landlord refuse to allow the tenant entry through his front door, demanding rather that he climb the steps to the second-story apartment, as he has contracted to do, and then descend to the ground-floor apartment, presumably through the hole in the floor? If the building is a three-story building, can the ground-floor landlord insist that a second-story tenant whose apartment floor collapsed, move to an apartment on the third story, or may the tenant reasonably object to being forced to climb one floor higher than he contracted for? Since many more issues may arise in a space-sharing situation (for example, in matters concerning privacy or safety), the Gemara is presumably only illustrating the complexity of the situation by raising a representative number of issues.

The Talmud refuses to give definitive answers to these questions. Instead it closes its discussion with the Aramaic word *teyku*, an abbreviation of the word *teykum*, literally meaning, "Let it (or these) stand unanswered." Tradition has interpreted the word as an acronym standing for *Tishbi yetaretz kushiyot u-va'ayot*: the Tishbite, Elijah the Prophet, will arrive just before the advent of the Messiah, and resolve all unanswered legal difficulties and problems. Until that time, certain legal and ritual issues discussed in the Talmud must remain unresolved, and we who live before the coming of the Messiah must strive to live our lives by compromising with each other, in order to prevent such disputes from turning into fights and quarrels. The final halachic ruling may turn out to be less important than the concept of tenant-landlord relations being codified by the Torah in the Talmud. Remember that even relatively secular, mundane rules governing human interactions rise to the level of Torah because we are constantly aware of God's image imprinted upon every human being with whom we interact.

The Gemara now concludes its discussion of this mishnah by examining Rabbi Yose's statement in the mishnah concerning the division of responsibility for fixing the hole in the floor. Remember, Rabbi Yose and the Rabbis of the mishnah disputed this issue. The Rabbis of the mishnah implied that the cost of materials and labor to repair the hole are the responsibility of the owner, but Rabbi Yose disagreed, noting that both landlord and tenant should each pay for part of the repair. Both the Rabbis and Rabbi Yose agree that the ground-floor apartment's ceiling, a thatched wooden structure (common in those days), is clearly the responsibility of the landlord. They argue over the plaster that coats this wooden mesh. Is the plaster coating merely a convenient way for the tenant to gain a smooth floor, therefore becoming his responsibility, or is the plaster an integral part of the ceiling/floor structure, in which case the building's owner should pay for it too? The Gemara begins by citing Rabbi Yose and then discusses the nature of the ceiling:

Rabbi Yose says: 'The lower provides the ceiling.' What is this ceiling? Rabbi Yose bar Chanina explains: 'Reeds and thorns (which formed a mat to be attached to the beams).' **Ustini explained in the name of Resh Lakish: 'Cedar wood.' And they are not arguing, for one rabbi explains in accordance with** (the custom) **of his place and the other explains in accordance** (the custom) **of his place.**

Sometimes in the Talmud, the law reflects the power of local custom rather than the imprint of carefully considered, top-down legislation. Even in our day, local authorities are often granted some autonomy with regard to ruling upon issues of communal importance. Building codes may be one of these issues, since the strength needed by a structure may depend upon local factors (such as, climactic conditions, and the risk of earthquakes or floods). Rabbi Yose bar Chanina explains the ceiling consists of one type of material, and Resh Lakish insists it is composed of a different material. The Talmud suggests both rabbis are correct, since each opinion reflects local custom. Therefore, how the ceiling must be fixed depends upon variations in local building codes. The yardstick for compliance is not an unchanging, inviolable rabbinic definition of what a ceiling is.

We have now agreed on what constitutes the ceiling, but have not yet decided what role the thin layer of plaster covering the floor plays in the structure. Remember that in the mishnah, Rabbi Yose ruled the plaster layer was not an integral part of the ceiling, just a convenience for the upper-floor tenant, so he is responsible for replacing it. The Gemara now challenges the reasoning we offered for Rabbi Yose's position. Perhaps responsibility for repairing the floor/ceiling is based upon who caused the damage that led to the hole between the apartments. This new approach will be considered by first presenting and then comparing a seemingly parallel case, argued by Rabbi Chiya bar Abba and Rabbi Ila'i, concerning damage caused by water trickling down from an upper-floor apartment to a lower one.

Two people lived (in two apartments), **above and below** (each other). **The layer of plaster between the apartments deteriorated and when the upper one** (the occupant) **washed his hands** (water) **trickled down and damaged the lower one's** (apartment). **Who repairs it? Rabbi Chiya bar Abba ruled that the upper one repairs it. Rabbi Ila'i in the name of Rabbi Chiya bar Rabbi Yose ruled that the bottom one repairs it. A mnemonic device** (to remember that the latter ruling was issued by Rabbi Chiya bar Rabbi Yose) **is 'and Joseph** (Yose) **was brought down to Egypt.' Shall we say that Rabbi Chiya bar Abba and Rabbi Ila'i are having the same argument as Rabbi Yose and the Rabbis did? The one who rules that the tenant, living above, repairs** (the plaster) **is similar to the one who maintains that it is incumbent upon the damager to distance himself from the one being damaged, and the one who says the landlord, living below, repairs** (the entire floor/ceiling) **is similar to the one who says it is incumbent upon the one who is damaged to distance himself from the damager.**

Remember that we are trying to determine who is responsible for replacing the plaster that coats the repaired ceiling. Until this point we have assumed that Rabbi Yose argues that the upper-floor tenant should pay for it since it is only there for his convenience, like a carpet in today's homes. The Rabbis, presumably, disagree, arguing that the plaster coat is an integral part of the ceiling, and, therefore, the landlord's responsibility. The Gemara now suggests a different way of explaining what Rabbi Yose and the Rabbis are really arguing about. Perhaps, the dispute revolves around the question of liability for damages. Is the individual responsible for causing the hole also responsible for replastering? In a similar case, presented by the Gemara above, someone living on an upper floor washed his hands; water trickled down to the lower floor through the ceiling, causing a hole. Rabbi Chiya rules that the upper-floor tenant is responsible for repairing the plaster, as he caused the damage. Rabbi Ila'i rules that it is the responsibility of the one suffering the damage, the lower-floor landlord, to ensure that no damage be caused to him, so he should pay for replastering. We now try to compare this argument over the water damage to our original argument between Rabbi Yose and the Rabbis of the mishnah. Perhaps, they are having the same disagreement. To figure out whether this is true, we must establish whom Rabbi Yose sides with on this issue of responsibility for damages done. We can do this by searching for more background information regarding how Rabbi Yose relates to damages. To provide us with this information, the Gemara now cites another dispute involving Rabbi Yose:

And do you think that Rabbi Yose and the Rabbis disagree regarding damages in these two cases? But we have heard them adopt exactly opposite views in another mishnah (*Bava Batra* 25b): '(The Rabbis ruled) a tree must be distanced twenty-five *amos* (cubits, a measure of distance in the Talmud) from a (neighbor's) pit (or well), and a carob or sycamore tree, fifty *amos* (so that the tree roots

**will not breach the walls of the well and destroy it),
whether (the well) is on a higher plane or on the same
one** (as the tree). **If the pit was there first, he** (the owner
of the tree) **chops** (down the tree), **and he** (the owner of
the well) **gives him** (the tree's owner) **money. If the tree
was there first, he need not chop** (it down). **In a case where
we are unsure whether this was first** (the tree) **or that
was first** (the well), **he need not chop** (it down). **Rabbi
Yose rules that even if the well was there before the tree,
he need not chop** (it down) **because this one may dig
within his own** (property), **and this one may plant within
his own** (property). **Thus, Rabbi Yose maintains that the
one being damaged must distance himself** (from the
damager), **and the Rabbis contend the damager must
distance himself** (from causing damage).

In the mishnah from tractate *Bava Batra*, the case presented
describes a tree whose roots grew across a property line to damage a
neighboring underground well. Is the owner of the tree responsible
for the damage his roots caused as it crossed a property line to damage
his neighbor's well, or is he not? In the mishnah, the Rabbis and
Rabbi Yose adopt opposing positions. The Rabbis contend that a tree
should not be planted so close to a well that the roots are likely to
breach its walls, and that one must carefully choose the type of tree
one plants, since different trees have different root systems. However,
even the Rabbis agree that if the well was dug after the tree had been
planted, the well's owner bears full financial responsibility for any
damage the tree caused him. Rabbi Yose disagrees, maintaining that
everyone has the right to do whatever he wishes on his property.
The potential damagee must take steps to protect himself.

Applying Rabbi Yose and the Rabbis' rulings in *Bava Batra* to our
case of the water trickling downstairs, clearly, if this is the case in
the mishnah, Rabbi Yose would place the onus upon the ground-

floor tenant to protect himself by repairing the ceiling, for he must protect his property from suffering damage. However, in our mishnah, Rabbi Yose rules that the upper-floor tenant must pay for the replastering, so clearly the dispute between the Rabbis and Rabbi Yose in our mishnah is not based upon their approaches to damages. If so, what is the basis for their argument?

Before answering this question the Gemara tangentially explains that the dispute between Rabbi Chiya bar Abba and R. Ila'i in the name of Rabbi Chiya bar Yose, which without a doubt is about damages, does echo the argument between the Rabbis and Rabbi Yose concerning damages in *Bava Batra*:

> **Rather, it is possible to say they disagree** (concerning the same argument as other Rabbis did before them); **they re-enact the dispute between Rabbi Yose and the Rabbis there** (in *Bava Batra*).

The Gemara then returns to searching for the basis of the argument between the Rabbis and Rabbi Yose in our mishnah:

> **As for Rabbi Yose and the Rabbis in our mishnah, what was their point of disagreement here? They disagree over the ceiling's strength. The Rabbis contend that the plaster helps strengthen the ceiling, and it is incumbent upon the lower dweller** (the landlord) **to do so, but Rabbi Yose maintains that the plaster only levels out the tiny holes in the floor** (which is the responsibility of the upstairs resident).

Rabbi Yose argues that the upper tenant is not required to replace the plaster to prevent damage to his landlord; rather, he chooses to replace the plaster because this makes his own life more comfortable. The landlord is only required to provide a sturdy floor, not a smooth one, so the onus to replaster falls upon the tenant. This was our original assumption, and it seems reasonable and satisfying. However, the Gemara will challenge this assumption once again, based upon a comment made by a student, rebuff this challenge and conclude with its final say on the matter.

> **Is this so? Rav Ashi has reported: When we were students at the academy of Rav Kahana, we would say that Rabbi Yose agrees when** (damage) **is caused by his 'arrows'** (that the damager, having caused direct loss by force of his own hands, is liable). (Rabbi Chiya bar Rabbi Yose noted that his father in this mishnah was referring to a case) **where the water stopped for a while, and then it fell** (into the lower apartment. So it did not fall directly and, therefore, R. Yose also agrees that the upper-floor resident was not responsible).

The Gemara offers us another insight into Rabbi Yose's reasoning. Rabbi Yose taught his students that just as the archer has responsibility for the damage his arrows cause, even if they travel some distance before striking their targets, so too an upper-floor tenant would be responsible for water trickling down and damaging the lower floor apartment. This seems to contradict Rabbi Yose's ruling in *Bava Batra* where he rules that a man is not responsible for the damage his tree roots cause. The Gemara resolves this inconsistency by explaining that when the damage is directly caused by an individual's force, Rabbi Yose holds the individual liable. However, if the damage is not directly caused by the individual, as in the case where the water pooled for a moment on the floor of the upper apartment before trickling down to the lower floor, or even more so in the case of the tree roots which stop their growth from time to time before resuming movement towards the well, Rabbi Yose would not hold the individual liable.

Therefore, having been unable to find another reason why Rabbi Yose would find the upper-floor tenant responsible for replastering his own floor, the Gemara concludes that according to Rabbi Yose the plastering is merely done for the upper-floor tenant's convenience; therefore he, not the landlord, is responsible for replastering.

Ethical Insights: Sanctifying the Mundane

The Gemara, focusing on the issue of liability for repairing the hole, does not address issues of privacy and safety arising in this case. As mentioned above, the Torah and Talmud both discuss these issues elsewhere. The Torah addresses similar safety concerns when it legislates the construction of a guardrail on the roof of one's home.

"If you build a new house, then you shall make a fence for your roof, so that you do not bring blood upon your house, if the faller should fall from it"(*Deuteronomy* 22:8).

The Torah dictates that if one builds a house, he must construct a fence preventing anyone using his roof from accidentally falling off it. Rabbi Dr. J.H. Hertz notes in his Torah commentary on this verse that homes in ancient Eastern countries possessed flat roofs that were used for walking, sleeping in warm weather, entertaining and other purposes. It was necessary to erect a guardrail to prevent accidental falls. The Talmud rules that this guardrail must be at least ten handbreadths high. Failure to protect human life exposes the owner of the house to guilt in God's eyes, as if he had murdered the victim with his own hands.

In tractate *Shabbat* 32a, Rabbi Yishmael suggests that the owner of the building should not be held morally responsible for "this man was predestined to fall since the six days of creation, for even though he has not yet fallen, the Torah refers to him as a *nofel* [literally, a faller]." The question raised by Rabbi Yishmael is that since the Torah refers to the one who will fall off the roof as a "faller," perhaps his fate is to fall. If God has ordained his fate, can our guardrail really save him? Rabbi Yishmael answers his own question: "Reward comes about at the hands of a meritorious person, and punishment comes about at the hands of a guilty one." Even if an individual is fated to fall, he is not fated to fall from a particular roof. Every owner has the responsibility to build a guardrail so that if tragedy strikes at least the blood will not be on his hands. Rabbi S. R. Hirsch further notes in his commentary upon this verse:

> In all the weal and woe that happens to men through men two factors are active together, the fate which God has destined for the one affected, whether it is good fortune or the reverse, reward or punishment, and the free-willed good or bad deeds of the people who bring it about... God hands us over... to the good or bad acts of our fellow man on earth, as Solomon said 'the Great Master of the world ... hires fools and transgressors in His service [*Proverbs* 26:10]'.

Talmudic law views the obligation to build a guardrail as the basis for a host of laws obligating the Jew to ensure that nothing on his property is capable of causing harm to another. Although the Rabbis believe that "a man does not even hurt his finger below [on Earth] unless it is decreed in Heaven" (*Chullin* 7b), this does not relieve man of his obligation to prevent injury to himself or to others. Thus, in discussing this commandment (number five-hundred and forty-six) the author of *Sefer HaChinuch* (literally, *"The Book of Education"*) writes:

> The Sages, of blessed memory, forbade [many things] in order to keep people safe from injury and far away from harm, with which it is not right for a human being possessed of sense to endanger himself. It is therefore fitting that people should be on guard against all things from which it is possible to derive harm.

Hirsch concludes that when building a house, one must carefully consider all the potential dangers, now and in the future, so as to ensure that the house is a safe one. Forethought must be taken to eliminate circumstances that allow tragedy to occur. Anything less is negligence bordering on unintentional homicide, an offense punishable in the Bible by exile. The Talmud declares that human beings are always responsible for any injury or damage they cause, whether intentional or accidental, whether they were asleep or awake, whether they were caused by themselves or whether by their property. The harsh indictment of the owner of the house for what, after all, is an accidental death may seem severe, but at least the Torah sends a clear message: we cannot escape our moral responsibility. The Torah makes abundantly clear that contributory negligence, even when not directly punishable, is something that must be wrestled with morally. As *Pirke Avot* (*Ethics of the Fathers*) 2:13 warns: "What is the best path for a person to cleave to... one who foresees the probable consequence of his actions."

In keeping with this approach, the Talmud in *Bava Kamma* 46a quotes Rabbi Eliezer's declaration that "a dangerous bull has no means of guarding except the knife." The owner of a dangerous animal that always poses a clear and present danger to others (even if it is tied up and guarded properly), has the responsibility of ensuring that this animal can never injure anyone, even if this means slaughtering the animal and incurring a huge financial loss. Similarly, the Talmud quotes Rabbi Nossan in *Bava Kamma* 46a who asks, "How do we know that a person should not raise a bad [or dangerous] dog in his house, nor raise a poor [or rickety] ladder in his house? [We know] because the biblical verse records: 'Do not bring blood upon your house [Deuteronomy 22:8].'" Based upon this insight, the Rabbis require that swimming pools be fenced in. Rabbi S. R. Hirsch adds in his Torah commentary that the local civil authorities must intervene to remove any potential hazards, such as a weakened wall in danger of collapse, even if civil law would not have held the owner responsible had it collapsed and injured others. *Sefer HaChinuch* notes that a person must even be exceedingly careful to protect himself: "A man should not set his mouth to a flowing pipe and drink, nor should he drink from rivers or lakes, for he might imbibe a leech.... and so they [the Rabbis] likewise forbade a man to put coins in his mouth."

God ordains each human being's fate; however, the manner in which it might come to pass is undetermined. It is as if we live in a subset of the universe God has created, in which we have responsibility, but not authority. We must act as if each life depended on our care and attention, for it may well be so.

MISHNAH THREE: *Upon Whom Does the Obligation Fall to Rebuild a Collapsed House?*

(In the case where) the house (ground floor) and the (attached) upper story, belonging to two (people), collapsed, and the owner of the upper story told the owner of the house (lower story) to (re)build, but he (the owner of the lower story) did not want to (re)build, the owner of the upper story may (re)build the house (just the lower story) and live in it until he (the owner of the lower story) reimburses him (the owner of the upper story) for his expenses. Rabbi Yehudah said: 'Even so, this individual (the owner of the upper story) is living in the other's space (the rebuilt lower story), so he must pay him rent. Rather, let the owner of the upper story (re) build both the house and the upper story, put the roof on above the upper story (but occupy the lower-story apartment) until he (the owner of the lower-story apartment) reimburses him.'

For a brief discussion of this mishnah crucial to understanding the following Gemara, please see Part One page 18.

GEMARA

Rabbi Yochanan said: In three places Rabbi Yehudah taught us that it is forbidden for a person to benefit from another's property (without his consent). One (case) is that of our mishnah (living rent-free, see the discussion on the third mishnah in Part One). **What is another** (case)? **We learned in a mishnah** (*Bava Kamma* 100b): **'If one gives wool to a dyer to dye it red for him, but** (the dyer) **dyed it black, or black and he dyed it red, Rabbi Meir rules** (the dyer keeps the wool and) **pays the owner the value of the wool** (before it was dyed). **Rabbi Yehudah rules** (the dyer returns the wool to the owner) **and if the improvement** (to the wool) **is greater than the expense** (of the dyeing, the owner) **pays him** (the dyer) **the expense, but if the expense is greater than the improvement, he** (the owner) **pays him** (the dyer, only for) **the improvement.'**

Rabbi Yochanan discusses three occasions mentioned by Rabbi Yehudah upon which a person unjustly benefits from another's property at that person's expense. The first case mentioned is the one just discussed in our mishnah, concerning living rent-free in another person's property. The second case concerns a wool dyer who mistakenly dyed a customer's wool a different color from the one he had asked for. What is the dyer's responsibility to the customer? If the dyer keeps the improperly dyed wool and reimburses the customer the wool's value before it was dyed, as Rabbi Meir suggests, perhaps he has not returned all that he owes. The customer may feel (and, certainly, Rabbi Yehudah does) that while he has received the wool's value, he has lost the valuable time he spent finding the wool, and he will now lose further precious time searching for new wool. While the dyer has paid for the wool, he has gained precious time that he did not have to spend finding or purchasing the wool. Therefore, Rabbi Yehudah believes that the customer has sustained the monetary loss of his time, and the dyer has benefited from the customer's original purchase of the wool, without paying him for this trouble. The customer deserves compensation and the dyer is obligated to somehow compensate him for his time. Rabbi

Yehudah proposes a different method of compensation for the erroneous dye job, one that prevents the dyer from unfairly enriching himself at his customer's expense. The Gemara, forgoing an in-depth discussion of the second case, now asks what Rabbi Yehudah's third case is.

> **And what is the other** (third) **case? We learned in a mishnah** (*Bava Batra* 168b): **'One** (who borrowed money from another) **paid part of his debt and deposited his loan document with a third** (person), **saying to him** (to the third person), **"If I do not give you** (the balance of the debt) **from now until a specific time, give him** (the lender) **his document." The time arrived and the borrower did not give it** (repay the balance of the debt). **Rabbi Yose rules that he** (the third party) **should give** (the document to him, to the lender), **but Rabbi Yehudah rules that he should not give it** (to him).'

The lender in a loan arranged according to Torah law does not hold the loan document after part of it has been repaid. At this point, the document is instead given to a third party to hold. The reason being that the Rabbis feared that if the lender held the document, he could produce the document and demand full payment at any time, even though the borrower had already paid one or even several installments. Therefore the document is given over to a non-partisan, third party. In the mishnah cited by our Gemara, the borrower partially repaid the lender, and, placing the loan document in the hands of a non-partisan, third party, set a date for repaying the rest of the loan. The borrower specifically instructed the third party to give the loan document to the lender if the loan is not repaid by the specified due date. Once the third party hands the document over, a dishonest lender can legally claim the entire loan, even that which has already been repaid. Should this occur, the borrower will be required to repay the lender more than the original loan. Rabbi Yehudah, taking a principled stand against unfairly enriching oneself at another's expense, forbids the third party from following the borrower's instructions and handing over the loan document.

We have now reviewed the three cases Rabbi Yochanan cited wherein, according to him, Rabbi Yehudah forbids acts that will enable one human being to unfairly enrich himself by using another's property. The Talmud will now try to refute Rabbi Yochanan's claim that each of Rabbi Yehudah's three rulings was based upon his abhorrence of unjust enrichment. Perhaps there are other reasons why Rabbi Yehudah ruled as he did in each case. Remember that Rabbi Yehudah, having lived at the time of the Mishnah, is no longer alive at the time of the Gemara's discussion, so the Rabbis arguing in the Talmud are free to come up with alternative explanations for his rulings. Only two caveats bind them: (1) If Rabbi Yehudah explicitly explained his reasons, they cannot be challenged; and (2) The alternate reasons offered must in no way demand that the ruling itself be changed.

> **Why is this so? Perhaps Rabbi Yehudah did not go as far as saying** (that the upper tenant must pay rent for living in the downstairs apartment) **because of the blackening** (of the walls). **Likewise, perhaps** (in the second case when) he requested (the wool) **be dyed red, and he dyed it black.** (Perhaps Rabbi Yehudah ruled the dyer may not keep the wool) **because he deviated** (from the owner's instructions), **as we have learned in a mishnah** (*Bava Metzia* 76a): '**He who deviates has the lower hand** (is at a legal disadvantage).' **And** (Rabbi Yehudah's ruling) **in the case of one who repaid part of his debt** (is also inconclusive) **for this is a case of *asmachta*** (where the borrower did not expect to have his instructions fulfilled)**, and we have heard Rabbi Yehudah say: 'It** (an asmachta) **does not bind one.'**

The Talmud argues that perhaps Rabbi Yehudah forbade the upper-floor owner from living rent-free in the first case because a by-product of his living in the lower apartment will be blackening its walls when he cooks. Having caused damage to the apartment, he will then have to compensate the ground floor's owner. The Talmud argues that Rabbi Yehudah forbids the upper-floor owner from living rent-free downstairs because of the damage he might cause, not because by doing so he will unjustly enrich himself.

In the second case, the Talmud argues that perhaps Rabbi Yehudah forbade the dyer from keeping the wool in order to penalize him for having deviated from his client's instructions, not because Rabbi Yehudah was concerned that he would be unjustly enriched.

In the third case of the partially-repaid debt, the Talmud argues that perhaps Rabbi Yehudah forbade giving the loan document back to the lender because the borrower's statement that he would pay by a certain date was mere hyperbole, used to assure the lender that he would ultimately repay the debt. Such hyperbole is termed an *asmachta* in Aramaic, and does not reflect the debtor's true intent, for he expects to repay the debt on time. For this reason Rabbi Yehudah is reputed to maintain that such asmachtas are not legally binding, and this, indeed, might be the real reason why Rabbi Yehudah forbade returning the loan document to the lender.

Although we have found alternatives to explain Rabbi Yehudah's rulings (so we cannot definitively conclude that they are a result of his abhorring unjust enrichment), we are no closer to answering our original question about whether the owner of the upper floor can live rent-free in the ground-floor apartment until being reimbursed for his construction costs. But let us review for a moment.

To summarize, we have analyzed the predicament of the second-floor owner who must wait for a reluctant ground-floor owner to rebuild before he can rebuild his own apartment. What are his options? He can start by rebuilding the ground-floor apartment at his own expense and occupy it until the ground-floor owner pays him the construction costs, or he can rebuild the entire building, including his own apartment, and then live downstairs until he is reimbursed.

If the upper-floor owner takes the former path, we are unsure whether or not he owes rent for living downstairs. On the one hand, perhaps he should pay rent because otherwise he would derive unjust benefit from another's asset, or because he may damage the apartment by blackening its walls. On the other hand, perhaps he should not pay rent because the rent might actually be or, at least, might appear to be interest on a loan (the money he spent rebuilding acting like a loan granted to the ground-floor owner). Alternatively, he might not even have to pay rent as the ground-floor owner is already deriving monetary benefit from his living there (left uninhabited, an apartment deteriorates).

If the upper-floor owner takes the latter path, even Rabbi Yehudah agrees he does not have to pay rent. The Gemara reaches no definite conclusions on how the upper-floor owner should act, but the options have been laid out for a court to rule on. The Gemara has fulfilled its objective of delineating the issues and comprehending them.

So far we have discussed the situation where the ground-floor owner does not want to rebuild. The Gemara now addresses the case in which he agrees to rebuild, but wants to make some architectural changes. Can he make any changes that he wants? Likewise, can the upper-floor owner make any changes he wants in rebuilding his apartment? The Gemara presumes that they may only implement changes that will strengthen the structure, but not ones which will weaken it.

> **Rav Acha bar Adda said in the name of Ulla: If the lower one wants to change** (by building) **with unhewn stones, we listen to him, with hewn stones, we do not listen to him; with half-size bricks, we listen, with full-size bricks, we do not listen; to cover it** (the apartment in order to make the ceiling, with beams of) **cedar wood, we listen to him, to cover it** (the apartment, with beams of)

sycamore, we do not listen to him; to decrease the number of windows, we listen to him, to increase the number of windows, we do not listen to him; to raise the height of the apartment, we do not listen to him, to lower the height of the apartment, we listen to him. If the upper apartment wants to change (by building) with hewn stones, we listen to him, with unhewn stones, we do not listen to him; with half-size bricks, we do not listen to him, with full-size bricks, we listen to him; with cedar beams (for his ceiling), we do not listen to him, with sycamore beams, we listen to him; to increase the number of windows, we listen to him, to decrease the number of windows, we do not listen to him; to raise the height of the apartment, we do not listen to him, to reduce the height of the apartment, we listen to him.

The lengthy list presented by Rav Acha bar Adda in the name of Ulla boils down to the notion that either owner may make changes which strengthen the overall structure, and neither owner may make changes which weaken it. For the most part, the list covers potential changes in the quality or quantity of building materials used. Unhewn stones were thicker (and heavier) than hewn ones, and so were better for the lower story, but worse for the top one; half-sized bricks were laid in two rows, whereas full-sized ones were laid in one row, so that half-sized bricks were better for the lower story, but worse for the top one, and vice versa for full-sized bricks; cedar wood is more durable, but heavier than sycamore wood, so it is preferable for the ceiling of the lower story, but unnecessarily heavy for the ceiling of the upper story; fewer windows make a stronger base, which was better for the lower story, but worse for the upper story, as this would mean its walls would be heavier; a taller apartment on either level makes the structure less sturdy, while decreasing the height of one's apartment provides a more solid base on the lower story and a lighter apartment on the upper story. In each case, changes that strengthen the overall structure of the two-story building and cause the least risk to each owner are permitted.

Having discussed the cases where the ground-floor owner does not want to rebuild (mentioned in the mishnah) and where he does want to rebuild (raised by the Gemara), the Talmud now raises the next possible, logical permutation of our case. What if neither the ground-floor owner nor the second-story owner wants to rebuild? The only value to the property is therefore the land. How should the value of the land be divided? The Gemara discusses:

> **If neither this one nor that one has** (the money to rebuild), **what** (is the law)? **It was taught in a** *baraisa* (literally, external material; see commentary below): '**If neither this one nor that one has** (the money), **the owner of the upper apartment has no** (share) **in the land whatsoever.**' **It was taught in a baraisa: 'Rabbi Nossan says: "The lower** (apartment owner) **takes two thirds, and the upper** (apartment owner) **takes a third." But others say: "The lower takes three fourths, and the upper takes a fourth."'** **Rabbah said: 'Uphold** (the rulings) **of Rabbi Nossan, for he is a judge, and he plumbs the depths of the law.'** He (Rabbi Nossan) **reasons: To what degree does the upper one** (apartment) **devalue the lower one? A third. Therefore, it** (the upper apartment) **can lay claim to a third.**

A baraisa, sometimes referred to as an "external mishnah," is a mishnah left out of Rabbi Yehudah HaNasi's comprehensive edited collection of mishnahs, formally called the Mishnah. Less authoritative than the mishnahs that were included in Rabbi Yehudah HaNasi's collection, a baraisa may be cited to support an argument, but not to refute one. The issue our Gemara wishes to resolve is who owns the land under the apartment building. While opinions vary, as witnessed by the above baraisas, the owner of the upper floor seems to possess a minor share in the property, while the owner of the lower floor owns most of it. In practice, the final verdict may well rest upon contract law or upon local property law, but the Talmud gave the last word to the authoritative Rabbi Nossan, who both understood the law, and, as a sitting justice, was also well versed in applying the law to its human subjects: "Uphold (the rulings) of Rabbi Nossan, for he is a judge, and he plumbs the depths of the law."

Ethical Insights: Lending Money and the Crime of Sodom

The issues surrounding unjust enrichment deserve additional study. The first issue I will explore is that of the interest-free loan. Curiously, not only is a Jew forbidden to unjustly enrich himself using another's assets, he is also not always permitted to enrich himself using his own. The Torah declares: "You will not lend on interest... to your brother, interest on money, interest on food or interest on any thing that is lent. To a foreigner you may lend on interest, but to your brother you will not lend on interest..." (*Deuteronomy* 23:20).

Have any two lines of the Bible led to a more vile characterization of the Jew? As immortalized in Shakespeare's Shylock, a character in *The Merchant of Venice*, the Jew gleefully charges non-Jews exorbitant interest rates, while loaning to co-religionists interest-free. As Jews we perceive this stereotype to be a perversion of the written word, yet even the most favorably disposed "foreigner" may require an explanation of how we justify treating fellow Jews one way and "outsiders" another. How can we ask for equal treatment, as Shylock does, and yet refuse to treat others equally?

At first glance, taking interest seems like a fair business practice as both parties benefit. The borrower is willing to pay a fee to gain access to capital he desperately needs, and the lender deserves a return for allowing someone else to use his money. We all use this system on a daily basis. Whether we are buying cars or homes, paying college tuition or using our credit cards as a means of gaining short-term loans, we are constantly borrowing money on interest. This not-withstanding, the Torah prohibits one Jew from lending another money with interest no matter how mutually beneficial the process might seem to be.

The Rabbis of the Talmud felt so strongly about the prohibition against receiving interest that they extended it to include business transactions having any hint of interest about them. Thus, paying for goods whose prices may fluctuate if delivery is delayed was forbidden. Similarly, "buying futures" was forbidden because, as Rav Nachman noted in tractate *Bava Metzia* 63b, "any payment for waiting [for the return of one's money or the delivery of one's goods] is forbidden." Furthermore, the lender may not even accept innocuous favors from the borrower, such as a fruit basket at holiday time, or the use of a vacant room for the night (as alluded to by our discussion above), for they may be defined as interest. Only if the lender had received such gifts in the past before the loan was made did the Rabbis allow for exceptions.

The beauty of forbidding interest-bearing loans comes to light when it is juxtaposed with the positive commandment of lending money to our fellow Jews. The Torah urges us to make such loans in two separate places: "You shall surely lend"(*Deuteronomy* 15:8); "You will lend money to my people, to the poor that are with you"(*Exodus* 22:24). These verses gave rise to the *Gemach* (the Jewish Free Loan Society). The word itself, an acronym built upon the initial letters of the words *Gem*[*ilut*] *Ch*[*asadim*] (deeds of loving-kindness) stands for an institution as fundamental to the Jewish community as the burial society, synagogue or kosher butcher. Commercial lending institutions are created to make a profit; the Jewish Free Loan Society was designed to help people. Whether the loan is needed to open a business, support a family in crisis, or enable a bride to marry, it is freely given. The Chofetz Chaim, a rabbi who lived in first half of the twentieth century, describes supporting the *gemach* (Jewish free loan societies) as both a great *mitzva* (commandment) and as a way for the lender to improve his or her character. Thus, even without an interest payment, both the borrower and the lender derive benefit.

We can now understand the prohibition against interest. The Torah considers it unseemly for family members, as all Jews are, to make money off one another in times of need. Furthermore, the Rabbis ruled that "all Israelites are guarantors for one another"; thus, a Jew's obligations towards his fellow Jew go far beyond ordinary business concerns.

But what about the heinous charge of "shylocking," taking interest from the non-Jew as Shylock did in Shakespeare's *The Merchant of Venice*? Are the Jews guilty of this charge? Forgoing profit on a loan to family members does not necessitate forgoing legitimate profit earned in honorable business dealings concluded with others. Nor does it restrict us from offering interest-free loans to our non-Jewish friends who are in dire financial straits. And yet, the Talmudic commentators stressed that because of our need to create communities that include Jew and non-Jew alike, and as a method of preventing enmity from developing between us and our neighbors, we would be better off extending such interest-free loans to all human beings, no mater what their religious affiliations. As the Torah decrees, "And if your brother becomes poor, and his means fail in your proximity, then you will uphold him, proselyte or resident, will he live with you. Take no interest of him or increase, but you shall fear your God (*Leviticus* 25:35–36)."

Above, in our discussion of the Gemara, we studied the issue of how the Rabbis felt about someone living rent-free in another's unused apartment. I will now turn to the Talmud's extensive discussion of this challenge to our moral standards in *Bava Kamma* 20a–20b:

One who lives in his neighbor's yard without his knowledge, does he have to pay rent or not? What is the

case? If you say that the case is one where the yard was not for rent and the squatter was not in the habit of renting, then this one (the squatter) **does not benefit and this one** (the owner) **does not lose.**

In this excerpt the Gemara introduces the parameters of the case of the unused yard. If the owner usually rents the yard out, the squatter costs him money and should pay him; however, if he never rents it out, then the owner loses nothing by having someone squatting there, and so perhaps should not be paid. If the squatter does not need the place to stay, then he gains nothing by squatting, and so should not be charged for benefiting. If he would have rented elsewhere otherwise, then he benefits and should pay. The case of unjust enrichment primarily concerns itself with the situation where the squatter usually rents, but the owner does not usually rent out his yard. In this case, the owner loses nothing if the squatter stays rent-free as he never intended to make money by renting the place out anyway, but the squatter would gain, since otherwise he would have had to pay rent. The Talmud notes that the squatter can say to the owner, "What loss have I caused you?" while the owner can respond, "You have benefited, and therefore you should pay for having done so." The Talmud concludes that the squatter must pay for the benefit he receives.

Pirke Avot 5:13, however, provides a counterbalance to this logical conclusion of the Gemara:

There are four types of people. People who say 'What is mine is mine and what is yours is yours,' are average, but some say this is characteristic of the people of Sodom. People who say, 'What is mine is yours and what is yours is mine' are ignorant people. People who say, 'What is mine is yours and what is yours is yours' are saintly people.

And people who say 'What is yours is mine and what is mine is mine' are wicked people.

Why does one opinion in this mishnah describe what seems to be an average person's response ("What is mine is mine and what is yours is yours") as characteristic of the way the wicked people of Sodom behaved, a level of sinfulness so heinous that the Torah tells us that God had to destroy the city along with all its inhabitants? This category actually seems to exemplify the correct attitude to private property; what belongs to me is mine and what belongs to you is yours. The mishnah actually suggests another category for wicked people, those who greedily believe that everything belongs to them.

Apparently, the Rabbis wanted to make a point. Strict adherence to the code of "what is mine is mine and what is yours is yours" leads to a society with a body of fair laws, but one without a soul. While the squatter may be obligated to pay rent because he benefited from property belonging to another, if the owner incurred no loss by having the squatter there, perhaps he should demonstrate his soul and refuse the rent. An action like this would define his personality. The Rabbis explained that Sodom did not begin as an evil city; rather, the Sodomites aimed to be a city of absolute fairness, one where no unjust enrichment occurred. In their eagerness to prevent unjust enrichment, the people of Sodom became morally bankrupt, say the Rabbis; the people of Sodom slid down the slippery slope, fashioning for themselves a society where no one cared about anyone else. The Rabbis warned that one must always be prepared to go beyond the letter of the law in order to do "what is right and good in the eyes of God"(*Deuteronomy* 6:18). The laws of Mandatory Palestine ruled, as British law did, that unjust enrichment was intolerable, and benefit must always be paid for. The Israeli government, which based its initial laws on the British system, similarly legislated laws to require payment for benefit. But mindful of the lessons of the Rabbis, the

Israeli parliament included exceptions to be adjudicated if the unjust enrichment caused the giver no loss and the receiver could not afford to pay.

MISHNAH FOUR: *The Olive Press, the Unstable Tree or Wall, and the Worker's Wages*

Similarly, (in the case where) **an olive press is built into** (a cavern carved out of a) **rock, and a garden is** (planted) **on top** (of the roof of the cavern), **and it** (the roof of the cavern, partially) **caved in** (creating a hole between the rooftop garden and the lower level olive press), **the owner of the garden may come down and sow below** (on the floor of the cavern near the olive press), **until he** (the olive press owner) **repairs** (the roof, literally, builds a dome) over **his olive press chamber.**

If a wall or a tree fell into the public domain and caused damage, he (the owner of the wall or the tree) **is not liable to pay.** (But) **if they** (the authorities) **gave him a set time to cut down the tree or take down the wall, and one of them** (the wall or the tree) **fell within the given time, he** (the owner) **is not liable. If** (one of them fell) **after time was up, he is liable.**

Someone whose wall was close to his neighbor's garden, and it (the wall) **collapsed** (into the garden), **and he** (the garden's owner) **said to him** (the wall's owner), **'Move your stones,' and he** (the wall's owner) **replied to him** (the garden's owner), **'They** (the stones) **are yours** (to keep for the trouble I caused you, so you move them away),**' we do not listen to him** (the wall's owner). **In a case where he** (the garden's owner) **accepted** (the proposal to clear the stones as payment for taking possession of them), **and he** (the wall's owner then changed his mind and) **said to him** (the garden's owner), **'Here are your wages** (offering cash instead of the stones), **and I will take** (back what is) **mine** (my stones),' **we do not listen to him.**

One who hires a worker to work with him in straw or stubble, and he (the worker) **said to him** (the employer), **'Give me my wages,' and he** (the employer) **replied, 'Take what you did** (the straw you cut for me) **as your wages,' we do not listen to him. In a case where the worker accepts** (the straw), **and he** (the employer changed his mind and) **said to him** (the worker), **'Here is your wage** (in cash) **and I will take** (back what is) **mine** (the straw),' **we do not listen to him.**

Remember that this mishnah deals with four different cases and debates the diverse notions underlying them. For a brief discussion of this mishnah, crucial to understanding the following Gemara, please see Part One page 21. The first of these cases, dealing with a garden built on top of an olive press, will now be addressed by the Gemara.

GEMARA

(How much of) **a cave-in** (occurred)? **Rav says: 'A majority** (of the roof).'; **Shmuel says: 'Four** (handbreadths).' **Rav says: '(Where) a majority** (of the roof caved in the owner of the garden may transfer his entire garden down below), **but** (where) **four** (handbreadths caved in) **he may not, for a person can plant half below and half above. But Shmuel** says: 'Where only four (handbreadths caved in, he may move his entire garden below) as a person does not plant half below and half above.' And it was necessary (to repeat Rav and Shmuel's dispute from the first mishnah), for if we would have taught (this dispute only concerning the case of) the apartment (and not regarding the garden case we might have thought that) in that case Shmuel issues his ruling because people do not usually live a little bit here and a little bit there (in two separate places), but with regard to sowing (a garden), people do sow a little bit here and a little bit there. (Therefore) one could say that (in this current case of the garden, but not in the case of the apartment, that) Rav admits that his (Shmuel's) approach) is correct. But if it (the dispute) would have been mentioned in that case (the garden), (we would have thought) in that case Rav maintains his ruling (that the owner of the garden above should only receive an area equivalent to the cave-in below, because people can sow in two places) but here (in the case of the apartment) Rav admits to Shmuel's approach (being correct, that even if only a small area of an apartment floor caved in, a person may move completely into the downstairs apartment because a person can not be expected to live on two floors). So it was necessary (to state their opinions, even though similar, in both cases).

Normally, the Mishnah will not repeat itself without a good reason for the repetition. Principles learned in one mishnah are automatically applied to other similar cases, so other similar cases need not be mentioned explicitly in the Mishnah. When two similar-sounding cases are discussed in the Mishnah, we must determine what differences between them made it necessary to mention both. In the second mishnah in our chapter, we learned that Rav and Shmuel disagreed regarding the size of a cave-in necessary to grant a second-floor dweller the right to move into the ground-floor apartment. The case in our current mishnah, the rooftop garden and the olive press, seems to be discussing exactly the same situation; only the uses of the upper and lower spaces differ. And yet the Talmud repeats the seemingly identical arguments Rav and Shmuel made above, instead of expecting us to apply the principles ourselves.

In order to distinguish between the two cases, the Gemara introduces its discussion with the following rhetorical statement: "It was necessary." Since the first case deals with living quarters, and the second with commercial space, perhaps the two rabbis would address each of them differently. Perhaps Rav, who felt that one could live in two separate places, would admit that a person cannot be expected to set up his business in two separate places. Perhaps Shmuel, who felt that a person could not be expected to live in two separate places, would admit that people may work in two separate places, as evidenced by people routinely planting in two different locations. In order to dispel this potential misunderstanding of their approaches, Rav and Shmuel needed to repeat their arguments in both cases. So although Rav and Shmuel's positions remained firm, it was necessary to restate them in the second case.

The Gemara will now address the second issue raised in the mishnah, that of an unstable structure:

'If they (the authorities) gave him a set time to cut down the tree or take down the wall.' How much time does the court give? Rabbi Yochanan said: 'Thirty days.'

As we discussed in our commentary on the mishnah, this law comes with many qualifications. If the wall endangers the public, the building inspectors will give the owner thirty days to tear it down. During that time, should the wall collapse and cause damage, the owner is exempt from liability. If he fails to tear down the wall, and it falls after thirty days, he is liable. The inspectors reserve the right to demand the wall be torn down immediately if it is in imminent danger of collapse, and the owner must comply to protect his limited liability.

However, for the Rabbis this case was not simply about legal formalities. It was an opportunity to teach the people about the principle of going beyond the letter of the law, of living righteously. The Talmud in the tractate *Ta'anit* 20b tells us that Rav Huna exemplified this behavior personally when he daily inspected walls around his city. Finding one that looked near collapse, he would demolish it at his own expense and rebuild it for the owner, thus proactively protecting the public.

In tractate *Bava Kamma* 30a, the Talmud offers further insight into how to go beyond the letter of the law when building walls. In Talmudic times, builders commonly used glass shards and thorns mixed with mortar to build their walls. This allowed them to save money by recycling discards, and at the same time build solid walls. The Gemara discusses both the fiscal liability and civil penalties a person might be subject to if such a wall collapsed and caused damage. Since these walls were properly and legitimately constructed, the Gemara concludes that should they collapse, spilling glass and thorns into a public thoroughfare, the owner of the wall would bear no responsibility for damage caused by these dangerous building materials. However, the Gemara relates that the righteous would go to great lengths to avoid inadvertently causing such injury. Most would bury their glass shards and thorns so deep in their fields that even a plow would not unearth them. Rav Sheshet, afraid that someone might dig deep enough, burnt them. Rava placed them on the bottom of the Tigris River, where no one could be injured by them.

The Gemara concludes with Rabbi Yehudah's insight that anyone who wants to be righteous must study and obey the law of damages (including those laws found in our current chapter). Rava asks whether this is this really enough. Some people only obey the laws to avoid litigation, not to prevent injury to others. Surely the pious should do better than that. Therefore, he suggests that after learning the law of damages, a person should study *Pirke Avot*, a work teaching the ethics meant to complement and provide a foundation for the law and its interpretation. Such study teaches us not only how to live within the law, but also when to go beyond the letter of the law.

After discussing the mishnah's second case, the Gemara now analyzes the third paragraph of the mishnah, that of a wall that fell into another person's garden. The Gemara is particularly concerned with who is responsible for the cleaning up the debris. A word of warning: the arguments in this next part of the Gemara can be difficult to follow. So do not get discouraged, even after several tries. Knowledgeable students of Talmud will sometimes need help getting through a particular segment, and if the explanation is not clear, the fault will likely be mine. Feel free to move on to the next part if you are confused, and come back to this part at another time. The Gemara begins by quoting the mishnah:

(As the Mishnah stated): **Someone whose wall was close to his neighbor's garden, and it** (the wall) **collapsed** (into the garden), **etc.**

Remember the issue discussed in the mishnah: someone's wall collapsed, spilling stones into a neighboring yard. The neighbor tells the wall's owner to clear away his stones, and the wall's owner responds by asking the neighbor to clear up the rubble, in exchange for which he will receive the stones as payment. If the owner of the garden agrees, the stones may serve as payment. However, if he does not, the stones' owner must still pay for their removal – even if this means paying the neighbor in cash – because the garden's owner has a right to clear his private domain of another's possessions, at the other's expense. The Gemara's discussion begins at this point:

Since the latter part of the mishnah declares 'Here are your wages,' we are dealing with a case where he (the garden owner) **had already removed them** (the stones). **The reason** (the garden owner may keep the stones as payment) **is that he removed them** (already), **but if he had not yet removed them, he may not** (keep the stones). **Why is this so? His field** (his property) **should have acquired the stones for him** (even if he had not removed them), **for Rabbi Yose bar Rabbi Chanina maintained that 'A person's courtyard acquires for him without his knowledge.' These words** (of Rabbi Chanina's) **apply in a case where he** (the owner of the object) **intended to transfer ownership to him** (the owner of the courtyard). **But in the present case, he was just evading his request** (when he told the garden owner that he could keep the stones if he cleared them; he had hoped to evade the courtyard acquiring the stones for its owner, so that he would have time to remove them himself).

The Gemara analyzes whether there is any legal significance to whether or not the garden's owner had already cleared the stones away before the wall's owner retracted his offer. Basing itself upon the phrase, "Here are your wages" used in the mishnah, the Gemara concludes that if the stones had been cleared away, the neighbor may keep the stones as payment. If they had not yet been cleared away, the stones' owner may retract his offer. However the Gemara immediately notes that this ruling contradicts Rabbi Yose bar Rabbi Chanina's theoretical stance that the moment the stones fell into his property, the garden's owner gained immediate ownership, as, according to Rabbi Yose, a person's courtyard acquires for him. The Talmud responds that Rabbi Yose's position only applies if the stones' owner really meant to transfer ownership over the stones.

This argument raises a set of questions not addressed explicitly in the Gemara. What is the legal validity of a false declaration or offer? Can an individual make such a statement under certain circumstances, knowing that it is retractable? In the third mishnah, we learned about an asmachta, a declaration made in order to buy time or convince others of the debtor's sincerity. Although the debtor has no intention that his instructions be honored, this declaration is permissible under Jewish law. In our case, perhaps the wall's owner wanted to keep his stones, but could not clear them himself at that time. He only made the offer to the garden owner to buy some time so that later he could collect the stones himself. According to Jewish law, we take his real intent into consideration and until the garden's owner actually clears the stones, the stones' owner can retract.

Having witnessed the mishnah's debate over whether the garden owner can be forced to accept goods (the stones) as opposed to cash, in payment for removing the stones, the Gemara now addresses the case, mentioned in the mishnah, of a field worker whose employer wants to pay him in produce rather than in cash. Before beginning its discussion, the Gemara quotes the fourth paragraph of the mishnah, to refamiliarize us with the case:

> **(The Gemara quotes the next part of the mishnah): 'One who hires a worker to work with him in straw or stubble, and he** (the worker) **said to him** (the employer), **"Give me my wages,"** and he (the employer) **replied, "Take what you did** (the straw you cut for me) **as your wages,"** we do not listen to him. In a case where the worker accepts (the straw), **and he** (the employer changed his mind and) **said to him** (the worker), **"Here is your wage** (in cash) **and I will take** (back what is) **mine** (the straw)," **we do not listen to him.'**

Remember, we explained that the fourth part of the mishnah deals with the salary due a worker who helps clear debris. The mishnah discusses whether he can be paid in produce instead of cash. The mishnah implies that the employer can pay in produce only if the employee agrees. As noted in our commentary on the mishnah, by Torah law, the rights of the worker are protected by the commandment to pay the worker by the end of each workday. The employer must not delay paying him. Given this restriction, the employer may be tempted to pay using whatever of value he has on hand. The Rabbis have explained that if the worker is paid in goods or produce, he will have to go to the trouble of selling them in order to get cash, and he may be forced to pay a conversion fee, thus losing some of his rightful pay. Nevertheless, the Rabbis add that it may be possible to force the worker to accept produce when it is a foodstuff (like wheat or barley) in lieu of cash because the worker can either make immediate use of the food or can readily convert the food into cash at current market value. Some Rabbis argue that only ready-to-eat foods, such as bread, may be forced on the employee in payment; thus, wheat and barley, as they must be processed before being eaten, could not be used.

The Gemara begins its discussion by evaluating whether straw may be used for payment. Straw is not a foodstuff, and therefore does not fit the guidelines mentioned above for cash substitutes. The Gemara commences its evaluation by comparing this case (paying wages in straw or money) to the previous case (paying wages in stones or money). Since the principle in both cases seems similar, the Gemara asks why the mishnah needed to discuss both cases. In the ensuing discussion, the Gemara elucidates the difference between the two cases.

It was necessary (to rule on both cases, the case of the stones in the garden and the case of the straw as payment) **for if it** (the mishnah) **had taught only the first case** (where the wall collapsed into a neighbor's garden) **then when he** (the wall's owner) **says, 'Keep it** (the stones, if you clear them away),' **we do not listen to him** (when he says he would like to pay the garden owner in stones rather than money) **as they do not have a wage agreement**

between them (because the owner of the garden has no payment due him until he agrees to remove the stones and does so; therefore, the type of payment is not yet fixed). **But here** (in the case of straw, offered as payment for a day's work in the field), **where there is a wage agreement between them** (the employer owes the laborer payment), **one might say we do listen to him** (the employer) **for as the popular saying goes, 'From one who is in your debt, collect even bran'** (do not pass up the opportunity for any form of payment). **And if it** (the mishnah) **would have taught the principle here** (of accepting straw as wages, and omitted discussing the case of stones as wages), (one might have thought) **here, once he** (the worker) **accepted** (straw as payment), **we do not listen to the employer** (if he changes his mind) **because the employer owes the laborer payment** (and he accepted the straw), **but here** (or rather, there, in the case of the garden owner) **he is owed no payment** (by the stones' owner); **therefore, one might suggest listening to him** (the stones' owner when he changed his mind and wanted to keep the stones), **so it was necessary** (for both cases to be discussed).

Since in the first case, the owner of the garden can refuse to clear the stones (as he has not struck a deal yet with the stones' owner), presumably, he can refuse to be paid with stones instead of money. Extrapolating from this case, the field worker having already been contracted to complete work (for a cash payment), and having done so, should certainly be paid in cash. This notwithstanding, the Gemara argues that perhaps in the second case we would accept the employer's offer of paying produce because the laborer, despite having the law on his side, should consider the popular folk saying, "From one who is in your debt, collect even bran," that is to say, avoid unscrupulous business practitioners by getting paid as soon as you can in any way possible. Perhaps the worker even acceded to this notion in his head when the wage agreement was reached. Therefore we cannot extrapolate from the first case's conclusion to the second case's ruling, for it may be that in the second case the laborer cannot refuse payment in produce.

Had only the second case been presented, where we learned that if the worker accepted the straw, the employer cannot change his mind, than we might have extrapolated that in the first case the owner of the broken wall cannot change his mind either once the garden owner has accepted the notion of stones as payment. This notwithstanding, the Gemara argues that in the first case since the stones' owner never really wanted to pay the garden owner in stones – he merely spoke in hyperbole (using an asmachta) – clearly, as the mishnah rules, if the owner of the garden has not yet removed the stones, the stones' owner can change his mind. Since both cases present certain unique points, the case law cannot be extrapolated entirely from one to the other, and both needed to be discussed.

The Gemara now continues discussing the second case:

(We learned in the mishnah: When the employer says to the employee, 'Take what you did,') **We do not listen to him** (the employer, if he offers to pay the laborer in straw instead of in cash). **But we learned in a baraisa that we do listen to him. Rav Nachman said: 'This is not a contradiction for here** (in the mishnah) **it is his** (it is the employer's straw the employee refuses) **and here** (in the baraisa) **it is someone else's** (it is from someone else's field).'

The mishnah undeniably rules that the worker can refuse payment in straw, and insist on being paid in cash. This is what it means by the phrase, "We do not listen to him [the employer]"; we do not listen to the employer if he offers straw in payment. But here the Gemara cites a baraisa ruling that the employer can insist upon paying in straw. Don't these two rulings contradict? Rav Nachman resolves the apparent conflict by explaining that the two rulings apply in different circumstances. According to Rav Nachman, the worker can insist on a cash payment when he is employed in his employer's field, cutting his employer's straw. But, if his employer sent him to work in a field owned by a third party, his employer can, apparently, force him to accept payment in straw cut in the third party's field.

How can such a situation arise? The Talmud explains that in certain circumstances a laborer might be hired to work in someone's field (not the employer's) without the field's owner granting permission. The owner must still pay for the work done on his field once the work is completed. In Talmudic times, during the harvest season, this may have been a common occurrence, especially since the produce had to be harvested before it spoiled. If the owner had not made arrangements for the harvesting, a friend might make these arrangements for him. Under these circumstances, if a person hired an employee to cut straw in another man's field, according to Rav Nachman, the employer could pay the worker using some of this straw. The Talmud will now dispute Rav Nachman's explanation.

Rabbah said to Rav Nachman: In his own, what is the reason (why, when he works in the employer's field does the mishnah forbid the employer from paying the worker in straw)? **Because** (the worker) **can say to him** (the employer), **'You are liable to pay my wages** (in money).' **In another's field, he** (the employer) **is also liable to pay the worker's wages** (and, therefore, he can demand a cash payment). **For it was taught in a baraisa: 'If one** (an employer) **hires a worker** (to work) **in his own** (field), **and instead he shows him a neighbor's** (field to work in), **he must pay him** (the worker) **wages in full and then collect from the owner** (of the other property) **what**

benefit he gave him (whatever the owner owes him for). **Rather, said Rav Nachman, there is no contradiction** (between the mishnah and the baraisa) **for here** (the mishnah) **is dealing with his own** (straw, payment in straw collected from employer's field), **and here** (the baraisa) **is dealing with ownerless** (straw, payment in straw collected from an ownerless field).

Rabbah argues with Rav Nachman claiming as long as the worker is contracted to his employer and acting at his behest, he can insist upon being paid in cash, not straw. The employer must bear the burden of being reimbursed by the field's owner. Ruling in the spirit of the Torah law commanding payment of wages on time and citing a baraisa to prove his point, Rabbah argues that the worker need not bear the burden of having worked in a third party's field.

Rav Nachman responds by suggesting that the mishnah's straw belonged to the employer, while the baraisa's straw was ownerless (not cut in the field of a third party as Rav Nachman and Rabbah had assumed). According to Rav Nachman, while an employer cannot force his employee to accept straw in payment, he can instruct him to pick up ownerless straw as payment. The Talmud now challenges Rav Nachman's response by raising a different matter involving an employee working in his employer's field.

Rava challenged Rav Nachman (using another baraisa): **'An ownerless object found by a worker belongs to him.' When is this? When the employer either said to him, 'Weed for me today' or 'Dig for me today,' but if he** (the employer) **said to him, 'Work for me the entire day,' then the find belongs to the employer.**

The Gemara continues investigating the worker's right to appropriate wages and other income generated by him during the employment period. Rava, in challenging Rav Nachman's recent response, asks about unclaimed objects a worker finds while he is employed. Normally, by picking up a lost object, the finder automatically acquires it. But if the finder was working for someone else at the time he found the object, to whom does it belong? Rava suggests that the answer to this question depends upon the employment contract. If the worker was hired to do a specific job, such as digging or weeding, and the object found had nothing to do with digging or weeding, then it belongs to the worker. But if the worker was hired to work all day, with no specific job mentioned, than an object found while he was working belongs to his employer.

Extrapolating from this baraisa, if an employer hired the worker to gather straw for him in an ownerless field, the owner certainly acquires immediate ownership of the straw, and he cannot claim that the worker has acquired the straw on his own behalf. Therefore, Rava declares that Rav Nachman, in explaining the baraisa above, cannot argue that the worker owned the "ownerless" straw and, therefore, can be forced to accept it as payment, for the employer owns the straw gathered. Thus, Rav Nachman's distinction between the baraisa (where the straw was ownerless) and the mishnah (where the employer owned the straw) is refuted. Rav Nachman responds to this challenge in the subsequent Gemara:

> **"Rather, said Rav Nachman, 'there is no contradiction. Here** (in the mishnah), **the case is one of lifting** (acquiring the straw in an ownerless field on the employer's behalf), **and, here** (in the baraisa), **the case is one of watching** (or standing guard over the ownerless straw on the employer's behalf).'

Rav Nachman suggests another way to reconcile the mishnah's statement that the worker must be paid in cash, and the baraisa's statement that he can also be paid in produce. Perhaps, the mishnah speaks of work that involves lifting the straw and, hence acquiring it for the employer, in which case the straw belongs to the employer and the worker must be paid in cash, while the baraisa speaks of work that involves guarding a field of straw, in which case the straw is not acquired by the employer, and the employer can force the worker to accept straw in payment.

Rabbah questions whether Rav Nachman's assumption that guarding a field does not effect acquisition is true, for this was the subject of a debate among the Rabbis of the Mishnah:

Rabbah said: 'Watching (standing guard over) ownerless property is debated by the Rabbis of the Mishnah. **We learned in a mishnah** (*Shekalim* 4:1): **"Those who guard the aftergrowth of the** *Shemitta* (Sabbatical year) **take their wages from the Temple treasury. Rabbi Yose said: 'One who wishes, donates** (his time) **and guards** (or watches) **without being paid.' They** (the Rabbis) **said to him: 'So you say, but then the offerings will not come from the community.'"** Are they not arguing about this (whether merely watching an ownerless object can effect its acquisition)? **The** *Tanna Kamma* (literally, the first of the Rabbis in the mishnah to offer an opinion) **contends that watching an ownerless object can effect its acquisition, and if he** (the watchman) **is paid** (for his work), **yes** (then the aftergrowth belongs to the community). **But if** (he is) **not** (paid, then) **no** (it does not belong to the community, for the volunteer watchman will acquire the ownerless produce for himself). **But Rabbi Yose contends that watching an ownerless object cannot effect its acquisition** (so the Temple need not pay the watchman, he cannot acquire it anyway). (In such a circumstance) **when the community goes and brings it** (the crop), **then the community acquires it. And then what** (is the meaning of) **do 'you say?' This is what they** (the Rabbis) **said to him** (Rabbi Yose): **'From your words to our words** (based upon your opinion that the guard need not be paid, and our opinion that watching can effect acquisition) **the** *omer* (barley offering on the second day of Passover) **and the** *shtei halechem* (offering of two wheat loaves on Shavuot) **will not come from the community.'**

In the Mishnah in tractate *Shekalim*, the Rabbis discussed how the tax money gathered by the Temple was used to finance its administrative activities throughout the year. One of the functions this money was spent on was hiring a guard during the Shemitta year to ensure that the Temple would have barley and wheat with which to perform the obligatory omer and shtei halechem offerings. During the Shemitta year, the fields lay unplanted and anyone was permitted to harvest whatever crops grew (the aftergrowth that grew wild), even crops growing in private fields, since all produce was deemed ownerless. Fearing that the Temple might not have the necessary barley and wheat to perform the offerings, the Temple administrators set a guard to watch over a particular field.

Rabbah argues that according to Rabbi Yose, even if the guard volunteered his services the produce collected would be considered Temple property. Apparently, the guard's merely watching the field did not effect his acquisition of its contents. However, the Tanna Kamma contends that the Temple can only claim possession and offer the produce on behalf of the community if the guard was paid by the Temple. Otherwise, by watching the guard would personally acquire the crop, and then the offerings would be his gift, not the community's.

Rava said: 'No. Everyone (Rabbi Yose and the Rabbis) **agrees that watching ownerless property can effect its acquisition** (and so the watchman does acquire the produce), **but here they argue over whether** (having acquired them) **he** (the watchman) **will hand them over to the community unreservedly** (wholeheartedly). **The Rabbis maintain that we pay him a wage, because if not, we are concerned he may not hand them** (the crops) **over unreservedly. But Rabbi Yose contends that we are not worried about his handing them over unreservedly. And what is the meaning of 'you say.' This is what they** (the Rabbis) **said to him** (Rabbi Yose): **'From your words to our words** (based upon your opinion that the guard need not be paid, and our opinion) **that the worker will not hand it over unreservedly the** *omer* **and the** *shtei halechem* **will not come from the community.'**

Rava, in support of Rav Nachman's position that watching can effect acquisition, explains that both Rabbi Yose and the Rabbis in *Shekalim* agree that watching effects acquisition. They argue over whether the guard will be able to transfer ownership to the Temple wholeheartedly, so that the offerings are made by the Temple on behalf of all of Israel. The Gemara now goes on to explain that others understand Rava's position differently:

Some say that Rava said that everyone (Rabbi Yose and the Rabbis) **agree that watching ownerless property does not effect its acquisition** (and so the watchman does not acquire the produce), **but here they argue over whether we need to worry about hoodlums** (who will take the produce by force). **The Tanna Kamma maintains that the Sages decreed the watchman be paid four** *zuzim* (the *zuz* was a coin used in Talmudic times) **so that the hoodlums would hear** (that the crop belongs to the Temple) **and not take it. But Rabbi Yose contends that the Sages did not promulgate this decree** (for they were not fearful that hoodlums would take the growth). **And what is the meaning of 'you say.' This is what they** (the Rabbis) **said to him** (Rabbi Yose): **'From your words to our words** (based upon your position that the worker is not paid, he will not give it over whole heartedly) **so the *omer* and the *shtei halechem* will not come from the community.'** **And when Ravin came** (to Babylonia from the Land of Israel) **he taught in the name of Rabbi Yochanan that Rabbi Yose and the Rabbis argued over whether we need worry about hoodlums.**

Another explanation is provided by the Gemara for the argument between Rabbi Yose and the Rabbis, so the Gemara repeats both sides of the argument again. This time the issue of contention concerns whether the Sages promulgated a decree ordering the guard be paid four zuzim to deter, for want of a better word, ruffians from removing crops from the field. While technically the ruffians are allowed to harvest crops from the field during the Shemitta year, since all crops are rendered ownerless, and the guard does not effect acquisition by watching the field, the Temple needs to acquire this produce. Knowing the guard is there and being paid for by the Temple will dissuade such ne'er do wells away from taking from this particular field. According to this approach, the guard is in Temple employ, not to watch the field, but to very publicly establish a presence meant to deter ruffians from removing crops. When Ravina came to Babylonia from the Land of Israel, he reported that Rabbi Yochanan explained the argument this last way.

Unfortunately, having reached the end of the Gemara's discussion of this mishnah from *Shekalim*, we have not yet reached an indisputable conclusion. Rabbi Yose and the Rabbis might be arguing about something else. Likewise, our original issue – whether or not a worker gathering straw in an ownerless field, at his employer's request, acquires the straw and, therefore, can be forced to accept straw as wages – remains in dispute. Remember resolving this issue depended upon resolving another dispute concerning whether or not watching effects the acquisition of ownerless property. This dispute too remains to be resolved. Not all Gemara discussions end with indisputable conclusions. The thought process, itself, however, is of paramount importance.

Ethical Insights: Paying a Worker in a Timely and Appropriate Fashion Lest He Cry Out to God

This chapter emphasized the concept of paying a worker in a timely and appropriate fashion. The Torah establishes the law's fundamentals and tractate *Bava Metzia's* ninth chapter fills in the details. The Torah's legislation goes beyond a simple delineation of employer-employee relations; it teaches us what the Lord, our God, expects from us in our relationships with other human beings. In *Deuteronomy* 24:14–15, the Torah states:

> You shall not oppress a hired servant who is poor and needy, whether he be of thy brethren or of the strangers in your land within your gates. In the same day you shall give him his pay before the sun goes down, for he is poor and sets his heart on it, lest he cry against you to the Lord, and you will have sinned.

Since the Torah discusses similar or related subjects in more than one place, the Rabbis "cut and pasted" various sections together in order to provide a clearer overview of certain subjects. For instance, the Rabbis frequently created lists of related Torah commandments to gain insight into certain legal issues. By compiling compendia of Torah laws pertaining to business issues such as loans, contracts, acquisitions, and labor relations, the Rabbis created tracts dealing with business ethics. Compendia pertaining to positive interpersonal relationships, such as the obligations to lend and loan, speak appropriately, support the underprivileged, and give charity allowed authors such as Rabbi Israel Meir Kagan (the Chofetz Chaim) in his classic book *Ahavat Chesed* (literally, love of kindness), to create a model for society wherein all Jews share responsibility for one another. Books compiling the laws of daily ritual, such as Rabbi Israel Meir Kagan's *Mishnah Berurah* (literally, "clarified teaching") provide a single, unified text allowing us to clearly understand our daily, ritual responsibilities. These compilations seek to offer us both an overview and an in-depth analysis of subjects that would otherwise be harder, if not impossible, to learn properly, given that they are discussed in various places throughout the Torah and the Talmud.

Analyzing the quote from *Deuteronomy* above, we quickly realize that in these verses God decides to provide a reason for why this law was legislated. As you read the Torah on a weekly basis, you may note a number of instances where God feels that he must provide His logic for legislating a particular law. By uncovering these instances, we discover that in a number of them God legislated these laws to encourage ethical behavior, to prevent His being forced to hear the cries of those unjustly treated by their fellow men. Thus, in the quote above, we learn that withholding a day laborer's wage overnight is not just illegal, but immoral. God is not only legislating justice but also morality: "For he [the laborer] is poor and sets his heart on it."

Compiling a list of cases, we quickly discover a common thread. In the verses cited from *Deuteronomy* above we are warned to act morally "lest he cry against you to the Lord." Likewise in *Deuteronomy* 24:10–13 we learn that:

When you lend your neighbor any manner of loan, you shall not go into his house to take his guarantee [a night shirt]. You shall stand outside, and the man to whom you lent will bring forth the guarantee outside to you. If he is a poor man, you shall not sleep with his guarantee, but you shall surely return it to him when the sun goes down, that he may sleep in his garment and bless you...

For as the verses in *Exodus* 22:25–26 explain, "that is his only covering, it is his garment for his skin, in what shall he sleep? And it will come to pass that if he cries to Me, I will hear." Similarly, in *Deuteronomy* 15:9, when a Jew refuses to grant his fellow Jew a loan, God warns: "Your eye will look malevolently upon your needy brother, and you will not give him, and he will cry out to Me against you." And again in *Exodus* 22:20–22, we read: "And a stranger you will not wrong, neither will you oppress him, for you were strangers in the land of Egypt. You will not afflict any widow or orphan. If you dare afflict them in any way, for if they shall cry out to Me, I will surely hear their cry."

By juxtaposing God's words, we hear in God's own voice a crystal-clear message that He will hear the cries of anguish caused by our actions. Nachmanides eloquently summarizes this message in the following passage from his commentary on *Exodus* 22:20:

> You should not think that the stranger has no one to save him from the violence or oppression of your hands. On the contrary, you should know that when you were strangers in Egypt, I saw the oppression with which the Egyptians were persecuting you and I brought punishment upon them. For I see the sufferings that are inflicted by evildoers on people and the tears of the oppressed who have none to comfort them. And I free every person from the hand of violence. Therefore, do not afflict the stranger, thinking there is no one to save him, for he will be helped more than anyone else.

MISHNAH FIVE: *Placing or Storing Privately Owned Objects in the Public Domain*

(In the case where) **one places manure in the public domain, the placer places, and the fertilizer fertilizes** (immediately after the manure has been placed in the public domain, so no obstruction is created). **One may not soak clay in the public domain** (for the purpose of making bricks) **nor may one make bricks** (in the public domain, as the drying of the bricks obstructs the public domain for a long time). **However, one may knead clay in the public domain, if it is not for making bricks** (as just preparing the clay for mortar creates an obstruction for a brief time). (In a case where) **one builds in the public domain, the stone bringer brings, and the builder builds** (using the stones immediately). **But if he** (the builder) **caused damages** (because he stored materials in the public domain), **he pays for the damage caused. Rabban Shimon ben Gamliel maintains: 'The builder may even begin setting up his building materials** (up to) **thirty days** (before).'

For a brief commentary on this mishnah, see Part One page 24.

GEMARA

Shall we say our mishnah does not rule in accord with Rabbi Yehudah? For it was taught in a baraisa: 'Rabbi Yehudah said: "In the season when manure is taken out,

a person may place his manure in the public domain and pile it up every thirty days so that it will be crushed by the feet of people and the feet of animals, for Joshua distributed the Land (to the tribes of Israel) **with this stipulation.'"**

Our mishnah suggests that manure was one of the items allowed to be stored in the public domain, but notes that it could only be placed in the public domain for a short period of time so as to minimize public inconvenience. Therefore, anyone wanting to use the manure for fertilizer could claim ownership of it (as the original owner gave up claim to it when he placed it in the public domain); however, whoever claimed it had to remove it quickly, so as not to inconvenience passersby. The Gemara questions the ruling of the mishnah, noting that Rabbi Yehudah permits leaving manure in the public domain for up to thirty days during the season when manure is taken out. Rabbi Yehudah even adds that, in season, the owner may pile the manure up again every thirty days because people and animals walking upon it turn it into even better fertilizer. Rabbi Yehudah also teaches us that Joshua, Moses's successor, decreed this use of the public domain as a public right, along with several others, at the time the Israelites entered the Land. Joshua stipulated that only by accepting these rules regarding the use of public domain would the tribes receive their portion of the Land.

A list of the other rules Joshua stipulated appears in *Bava Kamma* 81b–82a. These include, amongst others, the public's right to use a pedestrian pathway cutting through private property, the public's right to benefit from a spring of water newly discovered on private property, and the public's right to collect wood on private property. These rules as a group suggest that Joshua was attempting to enhance the people's sense of brotherhood by limiting the rights of private property owners and setting guidelines for neighborly behavior. Thus, Rabbi Yehudah seems to believe that our mishnah is mistaken when it limits the amount of time manure can be left in the public domain. According to Rabbi Yehudah, everyone has a right to place his manure in the public domain for as long as necessary, so that people and animals will trample on it and create fertilizer.

Whether this right extends to placing any or all other objects in the public domain remains unclear. As well, the degree of liability the owner faces when he leaves his manure in the public domain remains in question. The Gemara will now probe Rabbi Yehudah's position to advance a discussion of the latter issue.

(No), you can even say that Rabbi Yehudah (agrees with the mishnah), **for Rabbi Yehudah admits that if** (someone caused) **damage** (through his actions, he is) **liable to pay** (for the damage). **But we have learned a mishnah** (which contradicts this assumption): **'Rabbi Yehudah admits in** (the case of) **a Hanukkah lamp** (left in the street) **one is not liable** (to pay for damage the lamp's flame causes because) **he acts with permission** (in fulfilling the rabbinic commandment to publicize the Hanukkah miracle).' **Must this not mean by permission of the court? No, by permission of a mitzva.**

How can a person be liable, if he performs a legally sanctioned action? The Gemara posits that the answer Rabbi Yehudah might give – in the case of the manure – legally left in the public domain, is that while permission is granted, responsibility comes with it, so liability applies. The Gemara questions this presumption with a contradiction based upon Rabbi Yehudah's ruling in another case. Rabbi Yehudah ruled that if flames from a Hannukkah *menorah* (Hanukkah candelabrum) left in the public domain cause damage, their owner is not liable. Since the Rabbis commanded the lit Hanukkah menorah be placed outside one's home, in order to publicize the miracle of Hanukkah, the owner has left it with permission. Thus, according to Rabbi Yehudah permission seems to obviate liability.

However, the Gemara questions whether we can compare these two cases. The Hanukkah menorah received the approbation of the court because lighting it is an obligation; the manure is dumped in the public domain to benefit only its owner. Thus, the different rulings in the two cases might not contradict each other because, in principle, Rabbi Yehudah might grant each owner a different level of liability. Having failed to determine Rabbi Yehudah's approach conclusively, the Gemara now seeks to explore R. Yehudah's position and this concept of permission versus liability a bit further.

But it was taught in a baraisa: '(Concerning) all these things about which the Sages said one may ruin the public domain, if he causes damage, he is obliged to make restitution (for what he damages). **But Rabbi Yehudah exempts him from making restitution.' Rather, clearly our mishnah does not follow Rabbi Yehudah's** (view). **Declared Abaye: 'Rabbi Yehudah, Rabban Shimon ben Gamliel and Rabbi Shimon all held that in every case where the Rabbis gave an individual permission** (to use the public domain), **and he caused damage, he is exempt from liability.' That Rabbi Yehudah held this way** (that he does not hold the damager liable to pay) **was proven above** (in the baraisa). (That) **Rabban Shimon ben Gamliel** (does not hold the damager liable to pay is proven) **by our mishnah where he said, 'The builder may even begin setting up his building materials** (up to) **thirty days** (before).' (That) **Rabbi Shimon** (does not hold the damager liable to pay is as) **we learned** (in another) **mishnah: 'If a person places an oven in an upper story, there must be beneath it** (an extra) **layer of plaster three handbreadths thick; but in the case of a stove, one handbreadth; and if he caused damage** (despite taking this precaution), **he must pay compensation.** (But regarding this matter) **Rabbi Shimon says that the Sages did not mention all these measurements,** (for any reason) **other than** (to teach us that) **if it caused damage, the owner is not obliged to pay.'**

Here the Gemara names three Sages – Rabbi Yehudah, Rabban Shimon ben Gamliel and Rabbi Shimon – who held that permission to act exempts one from liability. Proof for their holding this approach is brought from a baraisa and two mishnahs. Rabbi Yehudah is explicitly cited in a baraisa concerning "these things about which the Sages said one may ruin the public domain" as exempting one who acts with permission. Rabban Shimon ben Gamliel is presumed to support this position because he allows a builder to leave his building materials in the public domain for thirty days. (Admittedly, this proof is quite weak since allowing the builder to leave his materials in the public domain is not equivalent to exempting him from liability, if the materials cause someone damage.) Rabbi Shimon's support for this approach is substantiated by his ruling in a mishnah where a very heavy object (in this case an oven) is placed in an upper-story apartment. The Rabbis dictate that in such a case additional layers of plaster must be laid under the object to support its weight. If this "building code" is followed, but the floor caves in, Rabbi Shimon rules that the owner of the object should not be liable, since the Sages specifically set up these meticulous guidelines in order to exempt people who complied with them from liability. Having discovered three Rabbis who support exemption from liability, the Gemara seems to conclude that acting with permission, either in performing a religious commandment or even in conforming to a rabbinic ruling designed to benefit the individual, exempts one from liability.

The Gemara now turns its attention to another liability issue. This is a common Talmudic device: once a topic is raised, the Gemara takes full advantage of the opportunity to delve into it from many perspectives. Here the Gemara addresses the liability of a group of workers hired to build a structure. Their liability will depend upon the manner in which they were hired, separately or as a group. As you will note, this discussion of liability relates back to the issue of building codes we have been studying throughout our chapter of Talmud.

The Rabbis taught in a baraisa: 'When the quarrier delivers (the stone) **to the chiseler, the chiseler is liable** (for any damage to the stone or that the stone may do); **when the chiseler delivers** (the stone) **to the donkey driver, the donkey driver is liable; when the donkey driver delivers** (the stone) **to the carrier, the carrier is liable; when the carrier delivers** (the stone) **to the builder, the builder is liable; when the builder delivers** (the stone) **to the bricklayer, the bricklayer is liable. But if he** (the bricklayer) **sets the stone in the row** (completing the bricklaying process), **and it** (fell and) **caused damage, all are liable.' But it was taught in another baraisa: 'The last one is liable, and all the others are exempt.' There is no contradiction. In this case** (the second baraisa), (the individuals were) **hired** (separately to do their individual jobs); **in that case** (the first baraisa), (they were) **contracted** (as a group).

Who is responsible for damage that is the end result of a multistep process? The Gemara quotes a baraisa suggesting that each individual performing a step in a multi-part process is only responsible for his step. The minute he completes his part of the project and hands the product over to the next subcontractor, his liability ends. However, the same baraisa continues by noting that once the project is completed, everyone shares equally in liability if damage occurs. The

Gemara then asks: if this is so, why does another baraisa declare that even following completion, only the last subcontractor is liable? To resolve the question of liability after completion of the project (all of the parties sharing liability versus just the one who completed the final step being liable) the Talmud suggests we look at the original contract. Liability will depend upon the original hiring agreement. If, on the one hand, the homeowner contracted with individual subcontractors for every step of the project, then each one is only liable for the damage he personally caused. If, on the other hand, the homeowner contracted with multiple contractors who form a single group or are partners, then all the contractors may have some liability. A court will settle which concept applies in a particular situation.

While the Gemara addresses legal liability in this case, moral responsibility must also be considered if society is to grow and flourish. A model presented in the Torah for doing so is the law of the *egla arufa*, the calf with the broken neck (*Deuteronomy* 21:1–9). When a murder victim is found in the fields outside of town, the town closest to the body is determined and its leaders are commanded to bury the victim. The leaders of the town then go to a particular spot in the wild, slaughter a calf, and declare that their hands did not shed this blood. Why do they make this declaration? As the Talmud notes, no one suspects them of this murder. Why do they need to swear to their innocence? The commentators explain that the closest town's leaders must ask themselves whether they bear some guilt for this murder. Did the murder victim (or the murderer) pass through their town in need of food or work and finding none, go on to his fate? Did they fail to provide the victim with an escort? If so, even though the town's leaders did not shed this blood with their own hands, they may have created a society fostering murder. They may be one link in a long chain leading to the murder, a tragedy usually born of multiple fathers. Taking the Torah law of egla arufa as a model, each of the workers in a multistep process that resulted in damage being caused needs to examine his role, and legally liable or not, give thought to whether his "hands shed any blood."

Ethical Insights: Permission versus Responsibility Revisited

The issue of permission versus responsibility and subsequent liability is also raised in connection with one who runs and, thereby, causes damages in order to be ready in time for the advent of Shabbat (*Bava Kamma* 32a–32b). Does permission to perform an action (especially a mitzva) exempt one from liability for damage caused in the course of performing that action or not?

MISHNAH

> If two people were traveling on the public thoroughfare, one running and the other walking, or both running, and they injured one another, both are exempt (from liability).

At first glance the case seems simple: two people are traversing a public thoroughfare and walk or run into one another causing both bodily harm. The mishnah opens a window onto three possible scenarios: (1) Both individuals were walking; (2) One individual was running and the other was walking; (3) Both individuals were running. As both individuals suffer some injury, we might expect each of them to receive some compensation. In addition, we might expect the runner to have a greater degree of liability. However, the mishnah immediately rejects both these expectations declaring that no one is responsible for damages. Why is this so? While we might suggest that since both parties were hurt, perhaps the damages cancelled each other out, this seems unlikely. The mishnah does not specify that this is the case and the likelihood of both suffering exactly the same damages in an accidental collision is small.

Regarding the case where both individuals were walking, since both had permission to walk in the public thoroughfare, perhaps their acting with permission protects them from liability. However, in the case where one or both were running liability should attach, since no one has a right to behave unpredictably in the public domain, the runner should be liable. Perhaps this explains the mishnah's ruling in the case where both were running; they are both equally at fault, and, therefore, no damages are assessed. However, the mishnah's ruling in the case where only one was running remains unexplained. The runner should bear full liability, yet the mishnah rules that he does not.

Have we been reasoning incorrectly all along? Probably not, because logic dictates that the one running, who hits the one walking, bears full responsibility. So why does the mishnah exempt him? Presumably, even our mishnah agrees that runners, in general, who collide with walkers, do bear full liability. Therefore, the runner in our particular mishnah must have a special exemption that must be discovered. He must belong to a special subset of runners who are not liable. The Gemara – never wasting words – presumes that we have thought this all out on our own, so it begins its discussion at this point in our logical train of thought, searching for the subset of runners who would be exempt.

GEMARA

The mishnah is not in keeping with (the view of) **Issi ben Yehudah. For it was learned in a baraisa that Issi ben Yehudah maintains that the runner is liable because he did something unusual** (running is unexpected behavior in the public domain), **but Issi agrees that on Shabbat**

eve (Friday before sunset) **he is not liable** (to pay damages for running into someone) **because he runs with permission. Rabbi Yochanan said: 'The law is in accord with Issi ben Yehudah** (that running in the public domain incurs liability, unless the individual was running Friday before sunset).'

Issi ben Yehudah is cited in a baraisa ruling that while most people who run in the public domain are liable for any injuries they cause, those who run at sunset just before Shabbat are not. We have discovered our subset of individuals whose running in the public thoroughfare does not make them liable for damages: those who run just before sundown in order to prepare for Shabbat. The Gemara now analyzes our mishnah in an attempt to prove that it is indeed referring to this type of individual:

Our mishnah is discussing Friday before sunset. How do we know this? From the fact that the mishnah states that if both were running, they are exempt. Why do I require (this) further (explanation)? If in a case where one runs and one walks, he (the runner) **is not liable, why is it necessary to mention (the ruling) where both are running? Rather, this is what the mishnah meant to say: If one was running and the other walking, he** (the runner) **is not liable. When is this? When it occurred on Shabbat eve. However, during the week, if one was running and the other walking, he** (the runner) **is liable. If, however, both were running, even during the week, both are exempt from liability** (if they hurt each other because both are acting in a manner unusual for the public domain). **The Master stated that Issi admits** (to exempting the runner for liability) **concerning one who runs on Shabbat eve before sunset because he runs with permission.**

So it seems that if the runner was running in a last minute effort to prepare for Shabbat, according to this mishnah, he is exempt from paying damages. Again, we stand face-to-face with the question of whether permission (particularly, permission to do a mitzva) exempts the doer from paying damages if in performing the act (or mitzva) damages are caused.

The Mishnah discusses the case of a camel carrying straw on its back through the public domain. While the camel's owner is allowed to lead it through the public domain, if the straw catches fire from a candle inside a shop and burns down the shop and its environs, the owner of the camel is liable. However, if the candle was outside the shop and the straw caught fire, the shopkeeper is responsible for the resulting damage as he should not have placed his candle in the public domain.

Above we discussed the obligation to display the Hanukkah menorah in public view, in order to publicize the miracle it represents. By Jewish law, shopkeepers were not only permitted but obligated to place the menorah outside next to their stores. The Mishnah reports that if the camel's straw caught fire from a menorah placed outside, the shopkeeper was not liable. Likewise, perhaps the Shabbat eve runner is exempt from liability because, as with the Hanukkah menorah, he was performing a mitzva. In this instance, the mitzva seems to have been finishing last-minute preparations for Shabbat, such as buying flowers or getting a haircut, activities forbidden on the Shabbat itself. In fact, this seems to be the case, for it explains why the mishnah delineates a subset of one type of individual who runs and is not responsible for the damage he causes.

However, the Gemara is uncomfortable with the notion that a person, even one acting with permission, may with rabbinic imprimatur run the risk of injuring someone else. It therefore modifies its explanation slightly:

On Shabbat eve, why is there permission to run? As demonstrated by the declaration of Rabbi Chanina. For

Rabbi Chanina said: 'Come, let us go out to greet the bride, the queen.' And some say, he would say: '...to greet the Shabbat, the bride, the queen.' Rabbi Yannai would wrap himself up (in a prayer shawl) and stand in place and say, 'Come, O bride, come, O bride.'

Note that the Gemara changes its tone. This is no accident. The Rabbis back away from attempting to justify running immediately before sunset on Shabbat eve. In fact, just the opposite, they seem to avoid the subject. Had the Rabbis intended to confirm that this running was a mitzva, doubtless they would have begun debating during exactly what time period running was permitted, and precisely which mitzvas one could run for. Does permission to run Shabbat eve mean the whole day, from midday and on, the time close to candle lighting, or the time until sundown? Is one, for instance, allowed to buy provisions, finish cooking, bathing, or mending Shabbat clothes? Instead of discussing these technical, halachic issues, the Rabbis shift their focus to spiritual preparations evoked by Rabbi Chanina's words. They probably do this because running is inherently dangerous, and they may be ill at ease with allowing such conduct. They would prefer the runner take his time preparing for Shabbat, and failing that they are willing to forgo some Shabbat pleasures, rather than condoning and even, to some degree, granting their approbation to such risky behavior.

Our responsibility in the eyes of Heaven and even in our own eyes is far greater than the responsibility demanded by the law. The modern day equivalent of running to prepare for Shabbat might be driving over the speed limit or running a yellow light in order to prepare for Shabbat. These are actions which may have no negative consequences, but which can result in significant injury, and even death.

Thus, I think that because the Rabbis were uncomfortable with running on Shabbat eve, they offered a different interpretation of such running: the running one does to reach out spiritually, to greet the advent of the Shabbat. We are taught by the Gemara that the pious Rabbis would actually run towards the setting sun to symbolically greet the Shabbat queen. We still do so, singing "*Lecha Dodi*" ("Come, My Beloved") every Friday night, using the words cited at the end of our Gemara, "Come, let us go out to greet the bride, the queen."

MISHNAH SIX: *Whose Garden Is It?*

(In the case where) there are two gardens (each owned by a different person), one above the other, and vegetables (grow out of the cliffside) between them (on the vertical drop between the two gardens), Rabbi Meir rules: 'They (the vegetables) belong to the upper (garden).' Rabbi Yehudah rules: 'They (the vegetables) belong to the lower (garden).' Argued Rabbi Meir: 'If the (owner of the) upper (garden) wants to remove his dirt (down to the level of the lower garden), there would be no vegetables (growing on the cliffside; indeed, there would be no cliff).' Responded Rabbi Yehudah: 'If the (owner of the) lower (garden) wanted to fill his garden up (with soil) there would be no vegetables (growing on the cliffside; indeed, there would be no cliff). Then, Rabbi Meir said: 'Since each of them can protest the other's ownership, we establish where the vegetables get their nourishment from.' Rabbi Shimon declared: 'Whatever the (owner of the) upper (garden) can reach and pick by stretching out his hand belongs to him, and the rest belongs to the (owner of the) lower (garden).'

For a brief commentary on this mishnah, see Part One page 26.

GEMARA

Rava states: 'With regard to the roots, no one argues,

they belong to the upper (garden). **What do they argue about it? With regard to the part that is seen** (the branches or foliage, and the vegetables or fruits growing outside the soil). **R Meir says: "Throw the part above ground after the roots** (the foliage and produce is nurtured by the roots, and so is owned by the owner of the upper garden)." **Rabbi Yehudah argues: "We do not say throw the part that is seen after the roots** (and so it belongs to the lower garden owner).'" **They** (Rabbi Meir and Rabbi Yehudah) **are consistent with their approach elsewhere, for we learned in a baraisa: 'That which sprouts out of a** (tree's) **trunk or roots,** (the tree having been sold by the landowner to a buyer who bought just the tree, but not the land it is on), **it** (the new shoot off the tree) **belongs to the owner of the land** (rather than to the owner of the tree) **according to Rabbi Meir. But Rabbi Yehudah says that which sprouts from the trunk belongs to the owner of the** (tree) **trunk, and** (that which grows from the roots, such as a) **a shoot from the roots, belongs to the owner of the land.'**

Rava starts off our discussion by stating that everyone agrees that the roots nurturing the growth under dispute belong to the owner of the upper garden since they are in his soil. The dispute between Rabbi Meir and Rabbi Yehudah concerns whom the growth from these roots (the fruit or vegetables growing horizontally from the upper garden's soil) belongs to. As in the mishnah, Rabbi Meir claims that roots and produce belong together, while Rabbi Yehudah contends that this is not necessarily always the case.

Proof that Rabbi Meir and Rabbi Yehudah actually agree with Rava's declaration is now provided by reviewing a different case of theirs, that of a landowner who sold a tree on his land to another. If a new shoot, which may eventually grow into a new tree, sprouts from the roots of the old tree, all agree it belongs to the owner of the ground, the original owner. But if the new shoot sprouts from the trunk of the tree, the Rabbis disagree concerning who owns it. Rabbi Meir argues that it still belongs to the owner of the ground which nurtures it, as he only sold one tree, not any new trees that might sprout from it; Rabbi Yehudah argues that since this shoot grows from the tree trunk and the tree was sold, any growth from the tree itself belongs to the new owner.

Now we can understand why Rabbi Meir says that the owner of the upper garden owns the produce growing off the side of the cliff. In principle he believes that anything that grows from the roots is legally attached to them. Rabbi Yehudah, however, thinks that a legal division between the roots and any growth from them can be made. From this additional case, we learn nothing except that Rabbi Meir and Rabbi Yehudah are consistent in their opinions, as described in our mishnah and as described by Rava. The Gemara now offers another similar argument between Rabbi Meir and Rabbi Yehudah in an attempt to resolve the difference of opinion between them.

And we also learned a similar argument in a (different) **baraisa concerning the laws of** *orla* (fruit produced by a tree during its first three years): '**A tree which sprouts from the trunk or the roots is subject to** (the laws of) **orla, according to Rabbi Meir. Rabbi Yehudah says that if it sprouts from the trunk, it is not obligated in orla, but** (if it sprouts) **from the roots it is subject to the laws** (of orla).'

In order to understand this case, we must first define the laws of orla. For the first three years after being planted, the fruit produced by a tree is literally considered "uncircumcised" (the actual meaning of the word "orla" is foreskin). Torah law forbids its use and prohibits deriving any benefit from it. The fruit of the fourth year may be picked for use, but must be taken to Jerusalem, some of it to be offered on the Temple altar, and the rest to be consumed by the owner in Jerusalem. After the fourth year, the tree's owner may freely use all the fruit. The Mishnah devotes a whole tractate to reviewing the laws concerning orla. In the interest of resolving the dispute between Rabbi Meir and Rabbi Yehudah, the Gemara now examines a dispute between them concerning whether fruit that grows on a shoot that itself is sprouting off either the roots or the trunk of a parent tree has the same orla status as the parent tree or whether it has the status of a newly planted tree.

Here we learn that Rabbi Meir is convinced that in this case, any new shoots that bear fruit, whether they sprout from the trunk or the roots of the parent tree, must be treated as new trees and, therefore, are subject to the laws of orla. This ruling is consistent with his view in the prior cases. Rabbi Yehudah distinguishes between a new shoot that sprouts off the parent tree's roots which is subject to orla, like any new tree would be, and a new shoot that sprouts from the parent tree's trunk that is only subject to orla as part of the parent tree. Thus, each rabbi seems to stolidly cling to his own approach without compromise, and we are unable to find proof for one or the other, in order to render a verdict regarding our original question: to whom the produce growing from the side of the cliff belongs.

The Gemara, like us, also tires of reviewing what was essentially the same case three times, and asks: why was it necessary to recount both of the second two cases if any one case would have sufficed to delineate the Rabbis' approaches? The Gemara then answers itself:

And both (cases) **are necessary** (to mention). **For if you would discuss** (only) **the first case** (the sale of the tree), (you might have reasoned that) **in this case Rabbi Yehudah ruled this way because it is a monetary case** (in monetary cases he would rule according to the letter of the law as with two parties financially dependent upon the court's ruling, we need to rule exactly), **but in** (a case of) **orla, which is a matter of** (ritual) **prohibition** (where leniency may be an option, as two parties are not involved in a dispute), **one could argue that he** (Rabbi Yehudah) **would agree with Rabbi Meir. And if we had only discussed the dispute** (as it related to orla), (you might have reasoned that) in this case **Rabbi Meir ruled this way** (stringently in the case of a ritual prohibition), **but in the other he would agree with Rabbi Yehudah. So it was necessary** (to discuss both cases).

The Gemara explains that since the case of the purchased tree had to do with monetary law and the case of orla had to do with ritual law, we were concerned that each rabbi might have reversed his opinion in the other case. For, on the one hand, monetary disputes usually demand a verdict in consonance with the letter of the law because either lenient or stringent rulings may injure one party in favor of the other; but, on the other hand, ritual issues allow, and sometimes even favor, lenient rulings. Therefore, either Rabbi Meir or Rabbi Yehudah might have reversed his position in the other case. To clarify that neither wavered even one iota from their principled positions, either in the monetary or ritual cases, it was necessary to discuss both cases.

We have now exhausted our attempts at determining whether Rabbi Meir or Rabbi Yehudah is correct, and so we cannot achieve our original objective of rendering a verdict according to one of them in the case of the mishnah. At this point the mishnah and the Gemara turn to Rabbi Shimon, who, thinks "outside the box." Looking at the situation from a different perspective, maybe he will come up with a convincing approach to determining who owns the fruit growing off the cliff.

Rabbi Shimon said (in our mishnah): '**Whatever the upper one** (garden owner) **can reach by stretching out his hands**

is his, and the rest belongs to the lower (garden owner).'
They said in the academy of Rabbi Yannai: 'As long as
he does not have to overstretch.' Rav Anan posed a
question, and some say Rabbi Yirmiya (asked it): 'If the
owner of the upper garden can reach the foliage, but not
the roots, or if he can reach its roots but not its foliage,
what (is the law)?' Let it go unanswered. Ephraim the
scribe, who was a disciple of Resh Lakish said in the name
of Resh Lakish that the law is in accord with the view of
Rabbi Shimon. They reported the ruling to King Shapur
who said to them: 'Rabbi Shimon should be praised.'

We now come to Rabbi Shimon's compromise. Whatever the upper
owner can collect by reaching downward belongs to him. Of the
remaining foliage that he cannot reach, whatever the lower owner
can reach by stretching upward belongs to him. There is some legal
precedent for this compromise. The upper owner's despair at never
being able to harvest the foliage on the lower part of the cliff means
that legally speaking he has given up on it, making it *hefker*
(ownerless). Once he gives up hope of recovering the harvest, by
law it is no longer his. Therefore, the lower owner can now legally
claim the foliage that the upper owner cannot reach. By applying
the notion of hefker, Rabbi Shimon creates a workable, compromise
solution. As the Gemara indicates, the other Rabbis commenting on
the solution (Ephraim the scribe and Resh Lakish) quickly agree, and
the issues raised by Rav Anan and Rabbi Yirmiya are not addressed.
The Talmud rarely ignores a challenge, but when it does so, it must
have a reason. Perhaps lacking a clear decision in favor of one of the
parties, it recognizes the need for a compromise.

Of interest is King Shapur's entry into the debate. King Shapur is
a non-Jewish Persian King, and yet he finds the Rabbis' debates
fascinating. He even expresses his gratitude to Rabbi Shimon.
Presumably, he is not grateful just for the pleasure of the discussion

and the clever solution to the problem. More likely, he is grateful to Rabbi Shimon for ruling creatively on a vexing issue, enabling a compromise that leads to peace. Such decisions are welcome in his kingdom, as they should be in any land that strives to use authority for the purpose of creating peace among humankind.

Ethical Insights: Trees in the Talmud

In this chapter we learned the laws of orla, the tithing rules for new trees. In order to observe these laws correctly, a method of determining each fruit tree's age is crucial. The Rabbis of the Talmud developed a system similar to that used today for racehorses. All racehorses born over the course of the three hundred and sixty-five days preceding a specific date are considered to have been born on that date. The first mishnah in tractate *Rosh ha-Shana* teaches us how to calculate tree years based upon the day referred to as the New Year for the Trees:

> There are four New Year's days: the first of Nissan is the New Year for reckoning the reigns of Jewish kings and for establishing the order of the Festivals; the first of Elul is the New Year for animal tithes, but R. Elazar and R. Shimon say it is the first of Tishrei; the first of Tishrei is the New Year for reckoning the years, and for reckoning the Sabbatical and Jubilee years, the planting and the vegetables; the first of Shvat is the New Year for the reckoning of tree years according to Beit Shammai, but Beit Hillel say that it is on the fifteenth of Shvat.

Thus the New Year for Trees, according to Beit Hillel, whose ruling we follow, is the fifteenth of Shvat, one month before Purim and two months before Pesah. Every new tree "born," or planted, from one New Year to the next is considered to be one year old on that day. The day itself has become a minor festival day, called Tu BeShvat. The name, Tu BeShevat, literally means the fifteenth of the month of Shvat, as the word "Tu" is composed of the Hebrew letters *tet* and *vav*, which have numerical values of nine and six respectively, to total fifteen.

This time of year was chosen because by this time most of the winter rains responsible for the year's growth have fallen in Israel, and thus the trees' blossoms are the result of rain that fell before the fifteenth of Shvat, the previous year in a tree's life. As Rashi notes, by that time the sap is rising in the trees, the almond trees are abloom and cyclamen and bright, red anemones are growing wild in the fields. As *Song of Songs* 2:11–12 states: "The.winter is past, the rain is over and gone, the flowers appear on the earth, the time of singing has come, and the sound of the turtledove is heard in our land." We are halfway through the Israeli rainy season (which extends from Sukkot to Pesah).

The new growth of spring becomes a metaphor for the eternal rebirth of Torah knowledge, as it is transmitted from one generation to another. I, therefore, want to share a tree story from the Talmud as a way of bringing this chapter, perhaps your first completed chapter of Talmud, to a close.

The Talmud, in tractate *Ta'anit* 23a, relates the following story:

> **Rabbi Yochanan said: 'All the days of that righteous man (Honi) he was distressed about this verse (from *Psalms* 126): "A Song of Ascents: When the Lord brought us back from captivity, we were like dreamers..." He (Honi) said: "Is there anyone who sleeps and dreams for seventy years?" (Afterwards) he was walking along the road, and he saw a man who was planting a carob (tree). He (Honi) said to him: "In how many years will this tree bear fruit?" (The man said to Honi:) "In seventy years." Honi said to him: "Is it obvious to you that you will live seventy years?" He said to Honi: "I found a world with carob trees. Just as my**

father planted for me, I am also planting for my son." Honi sat down and ate bread, and sleep came over him, and he fell asleep. A rock formed around him, and he was hidden from the eye, and he slept for seventy years. When he awoke, he saw a man who was picking some of the carobs off the tree. Honi said to him: "Are you the one who planted this (the tree)?" The man answered: "I am his son's son.'"

This famous story, demonstrating Honi to be the original Rip van Winkle, is often discussed in the context of our obligation to future generations. In our own generation, this story takes on a particularly poignant and literal meaning. Most of us have participated in collecting funds for the Jewish National Fund (JNF) to plant trees in Israel. What a delight it is to plant such a tree, and then look up at a forested mountainside, remarking upon how trees planted by the *chalutzim* (early Zionist pioneers) a hundred years ago continue to flourish and benefit their descendants. The planting of trees serves as a powerful metaphor for the return to the Land of Israel. However, Honi's story still possesses an even deeper level of meaning. To understand it we need to understand a bit more about Honi, himself, and about the reason for his question.

We recite *Psalm* 126, the one that so distressed Honi, as a psalm of thanksgiving before reciting *Birkat HaMazon* (Grace After Meals) on Shabbat. The entire psalm is as follows:

A Song of Ascents: When the Eternal returns the captivity of Zion, we will be like dreamers. Our mouths will be filled with laughter and our tongues with glad song. The other nations will say: 'The Eternal has done great things for them.' The Eternal has done great things for us, and we were gladdened. Restore our good fortune, O Eternal, as dry streams that flow again. They that sow in tears will reap in joy. Though the planter may weep as he carries seed to the field, he will yet return with joy, bearing the sheaves of grain.

The psalm has a historical context: the Babylonian conquest of the Land of Israel in the sixth century BCE. Following their conquest, the Babylonians destroyed our Temple and, intent on repopulating the Land of Israel with captives from elsewhere in their empire, exiled our people with the intention of assimilating us into their local culture in Babylonia. We could become part of the Babylonian Empire. It was a very seductive offer, and very clever on their part. In this way, we would lose our own cultural identity and gain theirs, never to rebel again. How did our nation, generation after generation, retain its identity under such pressures? *Psalms* 137, the Jewish people's promise to itself during the Babylonian exile, provides us with part of the answer:

By the rivers of Babylon we sat and wept as we remembered Zion. On the willows within it we hung our lyres. There our captors requested words of song from us, with our lyres playing joyous music, saying, 'Sing to us from Zion's song.' How can we sing the song of God upon alien soil? If I forget you, O Jerusalem, let my right hand forget its skill. Let my tongue adhere to my palate if I fail to recall you, if I fail to elevate Jerusalem above my foremost joy.

The Jews promise to teach not only themselves but also their children – offspring who have never even seen the magnificent Temple or lived in Israel – one simple message: do not forget. The Babylonian nightlife may appear attractive, but do not forget. A mere seventy years later the Babylonians were defeated by the Persians. When the Persians offered us the opportunity to return and resettle our land, as the psalmist writes, "we were like dreamers." The seventy years that Honi slept were symbolic of these seventy years spent asleep in exile. Honi asks the old man how it was possible for a people to hold on to a dream for seventy years, even as one generation died out and another was required to take up the dream as its own. The answer seems to be that each generation had to do its part. The Jews exiled to Babylon successfully transmitted their dreams of Zion, for their descendants were able and willing to follow these dreams two and three generations later. The dreams of the fathers had become the dreams of the children. So we see it is possible for a person to dream for seventy years.

Honi lived several hundred years after the Babylonian exile. He must have known the answer to his question, so why did he ask it? Perhaps, he was really asking about the fulfillment of dreams in his own time. Honi lived in the Second Temple period, during the reign of the Hasmonean brothers, Aristobulus II and Hyrcanus II. He lived after the Second Temple had been rebuilt, after the Greeks had captured the land, and after the Maccabees had freed the land from the Greeks. He lived during the reign of the great-grandchildren of the Maccabees. He lived in turbulent times. The Temple had been physically restored, but was lacking in spirituality. Honi saw the form but not the content and wondered if the dream had died. So Honi asks his question, and God sends the old man tending his tree to teach Honi a lesson. Each person must concentrate on doing the task assigned him and have faith that God will aid in the fulfillment of the dream.

The story of Honi teaches us that we are not the first to live in fear that the dream might die. Our task is to plant trees, and trust that God will provide someone to pick the fruit. Studying the Torah, we plant our trees, and pray that the fruit of these trees will be eaten by our grandchildren. As we sit and study, we bear witness to the dream transmitted to us by past generations. And when we share that knowledge with the generations to come, we witness how it can be passed far into the future.

הבית והעלייה של שנים שנפלו נחלקין בעצים ובאבנים ובעפר ורואין מאן מרין מכיר מקצת אבניו נוטל ועולות לו מן החשבון: **גמ'** מדקתני רואן מכלל דאיכא למיקם עלייהו אי בחבסא נפל אי בחבסא נפל אי הכי רישא אמאי חולקן נחזי אי בחבסא נפל עלייתא אתברו אי בחבסא נפיל תתיתא איהבור לא צריכא דנפיל בלילא ולידוונהו בצפרא דפנינהו ולוחזי מאן פנינהו ולישיילייה דפנינדו בני רשות הרבים ואזלו לעלמא ולוחזי בריסת דמאנרתבן ולידי

הבית והעלייה: ולידן כרסות דמאן קיימי ט' ולידה דהכא פשיעא ליה דחליי בנפל לרשות רה"ר מייריה שכן רגילות הוא שאינו נפל בכלימוס בשה וברים בכא במהרא (דף ד') פריך פשיעא דלה נפל הכומל זהי של שעיהם ומשי לא נריכא דנפל לרשות דהר ויל משום דאוק לה הכא דמומחים כמל זה כמו בכל לה פרין ההם פשיעא דהוה מבוטל עליה לאוהמיה דומיא דהכא שנמנים לפניו כמהגך ועוד דיהם (ה) נפריך מתוך הסוגיא דספר פרק פשיעא : **לימא** מיהי היוכחא דר'י דאמר פשור ואפ'ג דטעמא דר'י ל'אמר משום דאוק ממונא בחוקת מריה ושכא ליקימנא וקיימי כריהיי לא בנהלר ח] שאליי של שעיהם שאין האחד מוחק יותר מחבירו מ'מ כיר חטיב מומק שאר ורונוז שהתהיי של לכך פריך פשיה ועד דבך אסואל (נפל דף רה'

תודה רבה
נ] רש"י ד'ה סיפא
מולק וכו' עד נזכה
וכו' מס נ'נגה אח'כ
נוסח מבינו: (כ) תוד'
דר לימי אליי דלך פריך
משום פיכן גשהתיי

הבית והעלייה: כנן שני אחים שחלקו אחד נפל בים ואחד נפל עלייה שעל נביו והאבנים של תומת הבית מן תקרת הבית התחתונה שהיא קרקעיתה של עלייה ולמעלה של עלין וריומה ולמעה של התחון : שעיה חולקם : הכל לפי (א) כנבנה שהאחד הוא נבוה מחבירו ובניו ופערו מרובה מזכה מטל הפירו מולקם לפי שאין ניכר איזו אבנים של עלין ואיזו אבנים של תחתון : רואים אלו אבנים ראויות להשכר אם יש אבנים שטודות של לבנים זה אומר שלימות שלי וזה אומר שלימות שלי רואין אלו אבנים ראויות להשבור של עלין אם של התחון והכל לפי המפולת שלא מתבו הבית מיתה וגפל תחתיו החותה במקומה יש לדעת מהחתמעת נפכרו ולכך

ש"א התוספ'

TRANSLATION OF OUR CHAPTER OF TALMUD:

Bava Metzia 116b–119a

MISHNAH ONE: *A House Collapses*

(In this first case) a **house** (lower story) **and an upper story belonging to two people collapsed. The two owners split the wood, the stones, and the mortar. And we** (the court) **determine which stones are likely to have broken. If one of them recognizes some of his stones, he takes them, but they count for him as part of his reckoning.**

GEMARA

Since it (the mishnah) **rules 'we determine which stones are likely to have broken,'** it follows that it is possible to figure out whether downward pressure caused the house to fall or whether it received a (horizontal) **push from above. If so, why does the first part** (of the mishnah) **declare 'the two owners split?'** Let's see. **If it was pushed and fell,** (when we investigate we will see that) **the upper story** (stones) **are broken. If it fell because of downward**

pressure, (when we investigate we will see that) **the bottom story** (stones) **are broken.**

It (the ruling of splitting the assets proportionally) **is not necessary unless** (the wall) **fell at night** (because then no one saw how the stones were scattered). **But** (even in such a case) **let us look** (at the distribution of the stones) **in the morning. But they** (the stones, in this hypothetical case) **were removed already** (by passersby). **So let us see who took them away and ask them.** (It is a case where) **people in the street removed them and left. But let us see whose property they** (the stones) **are in so that the other party will have to bring proof. But if the stones are in a courtyard belonging to both parties, or in a public domain, or if you prefer, in a situation where the partners are not particular about each other's property** (than where the stones lie is no proof of ownership).

'If one of them (one of the apartment owners) **recognizes** (some of his stones),' **what does the other** (apartment owner) **claim? If he says 'yes,' it is obvious. And if he does not say 'yes,' why does he** (the claimant) **take** (the stones he recognizes since both owners seems to have equal claims)? **Rather,** (the case the mishnah discusses must be when) **he responds: 'I do not know.'**

Let us say that our mishnah is a refutation of Rav Nachman. For we have learned (in the discussion of a case where one person says that) **a *maneh* of mine is in your hand** (a maneh was a monetary unit in Talmudic times) **and the other replies: 'I do not know,' Rav Huna and Rav Yehudah rule that he is liable, but Rav Nachman and Rabbi Yochanan rule he is exempt** (from paying).

Rav Nachman said elsewhere: 'For example, where there is a business (transaction) involving an oath between them.' Here too (in our mishnah, regarding the discussion of whose stones they are, the case also concerns) a business (transaction) involving an oath. As Rava said, for Rava said that (the case is one where one person says) 'A maneh of mine is in your hand,' and the other replies, 'Only half of that which (you claim) is yours is in my hand, and I do not know if I owe you the rest.' Since he cannot swear (regarding who owns the remaining half) he must (turn over the part he does not dispute, and) pay (the balance he questions owing, but cannot swear to).

'But they (the stones he recognized and acquired) count for him as part of his reckoning.' Rava thought to say according to the reckoning of the broken ones (stones). Thus, since the defendant said, 'I don't know,' he (his case) is weaker. Abaye said to him (Rava): 'Surely the opposite is true: the other one (who recognized his whole stones) is (in a) weaker (position) since he identified these (stones) and not any others; thus, he does not own any others; all the other (whole stones) belong to the other party.' Rather, continued Abaye, '(it must mean) that (they count only) towards his total of whole stones.' If so, how did he (the one who identified his stones) benefit (from his identification)? Where (the stones) were wider (and so of more value) or the clay (of which the stones were made) was of good quality.

MISHNAH TWO: *A Hole in the Floor*

(In the case of) **a house (ground floor) with an upper story (second floor), the upper story's (floor partially) caved in** (creating an open hole between the two dwellings), **and the owner of the building** (who lives on the ground floor) **does not want to fix it. The occupant of the upper story** (a renter) **may descend and live downstairs until he** (the building's owner) **repairs the second story's floor. Rabbi Yose says that the** (building's owner, living on the) **lower (floor) provides** (the material for the part of) **the ceiling** (that acts as a foundation for repairing the hole in the upstairs floor) **and the upper** (floor occupant, the renter) **provides the plaster** (to cover the foundation provided by the owner).

GEMARA

How big must the opening be? Rav says: 'Most (of the floor).' **Shmuel says: 'Four** (handbreadths). **Rav rules most** (of the floor), **but if four handbreadths, no, because a person can live part** (of the time) **below and part** (of the time) **above. Shmuel rules only four handbreadths, because a person cannot live part below and part above.**

What are the circumstances (in the mishnah)? **If** (the landlord) **said** (to the tenant), **'**(I am renting) *this* **upper apartment** (to you),' (the apartment) **has gone** (and that ends the obligation). **Rather, where he** (the landlord) **said, 'An upper apartment** (without specifying a particular apartment).' Let him (the landlord) rent another (upper apartment) to him (the tenant). Rava said: 'No, (the ruling of the mishnah) applies to the case where he (the landlord) said: 'This upper apartment, which I am renting to you, when it goes up, go up with it, and when it goes down, go down with it (that is, when it collapses, move down to my place).' But if so, why (does the mishnah) mention (the case at all)? Rav Ashi said: 'Where he (the landlord) said: "This upper apartment which is on top of this lower apartment I am renting to you," because then he pledges the house (lower apartment in support of) the upper apartment.' Ravin bar Rav Adda related a similar case in the name of Rabbi Yitzchak: 'An incident, concerning one person who said to another: "This vine which is on top of the peach tree, I am selling to you." The peach tree was subsequently uprooted. The case came before Rabbi Chiya, and he ruled: "You are obligated to put up a peach tree for him as long as the vine exists."'

Rabbi Abba bar Mamal asked: 'Does he (the tenant) live alone as before, or perhaps both of them live (downstairs together), for he (the landlord) can reason with him (the tenant) saying, "I did not rent to you with the intention of being evicted"?' If you wish to say that both of them live there (together), when he (the tenant) uses (the lower apartment) does he use it by way of the (ground-floor) door or does he use it by way of the ceiling (entering his own apartment via the upper floor entrance, and then descending to the lower floor apartment through the hole in his floor). Do we say it must be as at first, just as at first (he entered) by way of the roof (second-story entrance) so too now by way of the roof? Or perhaps, (the tenant) says to him (the landlord): 'I agreed to make an ascent (to the original apartment) but not to make an ascent and a descent.' If you accept the tenant's assertion, what if the building had two upper floors (to rent)? If the uppermost floor caved (into the second-story), the tenant (from the third story) goes down to live on the second floor (with the second-story tenant). If the second-story apartment's floor caved in, does the tenant go up to the third floor (or down to the ground floor with the landlord)? Do we say that the landlord can reason with the tenant that he accepted a state of ascent upon himself (and, therefore, must ascend to the third floor as he did to the second floor)? Or, can the tenant, perhaps, argue that he accepted only one ascent upon himself (in the rental agreement)? Let these (questions) stand unanswered.

Rabbi Yose says: 'The lower provides the ceiling.' What is this ceiling? Rabbi Yose bar Chanina explains: 'Reeds and thorns (which formed a mat to be attached to the beams).' Ustini explained in the name of Resh Lakish: 'Cedar wood.' And they are not arguing, for one rabbi explains in accord with (the custom) of his place and the other explains in accord with (the custom) of his place.

Two people lived (in two apartments), above and below (each other). The layer of plaster between the apartments deteriorated and when the upper one (the occupant) washed his hands (water) trickled down and damaged the lower one's (apartment). Who repairs it? Rabbi Chiya bar Abba ruled that the upper one repairs it. Rabbi Ila'i in the name of Rabbi Chiya bar Rabbi Yose ruled that the bottom one repairs it. A mnemonic device (to remember that the latter ruling was issued by Rabbi Chiya bar Rabbi Yose) is 'and Joseph (Yose) was brought down to Egypt.' Shall we say that Rabbi Chiya bar Abba and Rabbi Ila'i are having the same argument as Rabbi Yose and the Rabbis did? The one who rules that the tenant, living above, repairs (the plaster) is similar to the one who maintains that it is incumbent upon the damager to distance himself from the one being damaged, and the one who says the landlord, living below, repairs (the entire floor/ceiling) is similar to the one who says it is incumbent upon the one who is damaged to distance himself from the damager.

And do you think that Rabbi Yose and the Rabbis disagree regarding damages in these two cases? But we have heard them adopt exactly opposite views in another mishnah (*Bava Batra* 25b): '(The Rabbis ruled) a tree must be distanced twenty-five *amos* (cubits, a measure of distance in the Talmud) from a (neighbor's) pit (or well), and a carob or sycamore tree, fifty amos (so that the tree roots will not breach the walls of the well and destroy it), whether (the well) is on a higher plane or on the same one (as the tree). If the pit was there first, he (the owner of the tree) chops (down the tree), and he (the owner of the well) gives him (the tree's owner) money. If the tree was there first, he need not chop (it down). In a case where we are unsure whether this was first (the tree) or that was first (the well), he need not chop (it down). Rabbi Yose rules that even if the well was there before the tree, he need not chop (it down) because this one may dig within his own (property), and this one may plant within his own (property). Thus, Rabbi Yose maintains that the one being damaged must distance himself (from the damager), and the Rabbis contend the damager must distance himself (from causing damage).

Rather, it is possible to say they disagree (concerning the same argument as other Rabbis did before them); they re-enact the dispute between Rabbi Yose and the Rabbis there (in *Bava Batra*).

As for Rabbi Yose and the Rabbis in our mishnah, what was their point of disagreement here? They disagree over the ceiling's strength. The Rabbis contend that the plaster helps strengthen the ceiling, and it is incumbent upon the lower dweller (the landlord) to do so, but Rabbi Yose maintains that the plaster only levels out the tiny holes in the floor (which is the responsibility of the upstairs resident).

Is this so? Rav Ashi has reported: When we were students at the academy of Rav Kahana, we would say that Rabbi Yose agrees when (damage) is caused by his 'arrows' (that the damager, having caused direct loss by force of his own hands, is liable). (Rabbi Chiya bar Rabbi Yose noted that his father in this mishnah was referring to a case) where the water stopped for a while, and then it fell (into the lower apartment. So it did not fall directly and, therefore, R. Yose also agrees that the upper-floor resident was not responsible).

MISHNAH THREE: *Upon Whom Does the Obligation Fall to Rebuild a Collapsed House?*

(In the case where) the house (ground floor) and the (attached) upper story, belonging to two (people), collapsed, and the owner of the upper story told the owner of the house (lower story) to (re)build, but he (the owner of the lower story) did not want to (re)build, the owner of the upper story may (re)build the house (just the lower story) and live in it until he (the owner of the lower story) reimburses him (the owner of the upper story) for his expenses. Rabbi Yehudah said: 'Even so, this individual (the owner of the upper story) is living in the other's space (the rebuilt lower story), so he must pay him rent. Rather, let the owner of the upper story (re) build both the house and the upper story, put the roof on above the upper story (but occupy the lower-story apartment) until he (the owner of the lower-story apartment) reimburses him.'

GEMARA

Rabbi Yochanan said: In three places Rabbi Yehudah taught us that it is forbidden for a person to benefit from another's property (without his consent). One (case) is that of our mishnah (living rent-free, see the discussion on the third mishnah in Part One). What is another (case)? We learned in a mishnah (*Bava Kamma* 100b): 'If one gives wool to a dyer to dye it red for him, but (the dyer)

dyed it black, or black and he dyed it red, Rabbi Meir rules (the dyer keeps the wool and) **pays the owner the value of the wool** (before it was dyed). **Rabbi Yehudah rules** (the dyer returns the wool to the owner) **and if the improvement** (to the wool) **is greater than the expense** (of the dyeing, the owner) **pays him** (the dyer) **the expense, but if the expense is greater than the improvement, he** (the owner) **pays him** (the dyer, only for) **the improvement.'**

And what is the other (third) **case? We learned in a mishnah** (*Bava Batra* 168b): **'One** (who borrowed money from another) **paid part of his debt and deposited his loan document with a third** (person), **saying to him** (to the third person), **"If I do not give you** (the balance of the debt) **from now until a specific time, give him** (the lender) **his document." The time arrived and the borrower did not give it** (repay the balance of the debt). **Rabbi Yose rules that he** (the third party) **should give** (the document to him, to the lender), **but Rabbi Yehudah rules that he should not give it** (to him).'

Why is this so? Perhaps Rabbi Yehudah did not go as far as saying (that the upper tenant must pay rent for living in the downstairs apartment) **because of the blackening** (of the walls). **Likewise, perhaps** (in the second case when) he requested (the wool) **be dyed red, and he dyed it black.** (Perhaps Rabbi Yehudah ruled the dyer may not keep the wool) **because he deviated** (from the owner's instructions), **as we have learned in a mishnah** (*Bava Metzia* 76a): **'He who deviates has the lower hand** (is at a legal disadvantage).' **And** (Rabbi Yehudah's ruling) **in the case of one who repaid part of his debt** (is also inconclusive) **for this is a case of** *asmachta* (where the borrower did not expect to have his instructions fulfilled), **and we have**

heard Rabbi Yehudah say: 'It (an asmachta) **does not bind one.**'

Rav Acha bar Adda said in the name of Ulla: **If the lower one wants to change** (by building) **with unhewn stones, we listen to him, with hewn stones, we do not listen to him; with half-size bricks, we listen, with full-size bricks, we do not listen; to cover it** (the apartment in order to make the ceiling, with beams of) **cedar wood, we listen to him, to cover it** (the apartment, with beams of) **sycamore, we do not listen to him; to decrease the number of windows, we listen to him, to increase the number of windows, we do not listen to him; to raise the height of the apartment, we do not listen to him, to lower the height of the apartment, we listen to him. If the upper apartment wants to change** (by building) **with hewn stones, we listen to him, with unhewn stones, we do not listen to him; with half-size bricks, we do not listen to him, with full-size bricks, we listen to him; with cedar beams** (for his ceiling), **we do not listen to him, with sycamore beams, we listen to him; to increase the number of windows, we listen to him, to decrease the number of windows, we do not listen to him; to raise the height of the apartment, we do not listen to him, to reduce the height of the apartment, we listen to him.**

If neither this one nor that one has (the money to rebuild), **what** (is the law)? **It was taught in a baraisa: 'If neither this one nor that one has** (the money), **the owner of the upper apartment has no** (share) **in the land whatsoever.'** **It was taught in a baraisa: 'Rabbi Nossan says: "The lower** (apartment owner) **takes two thirds, and the upper** (apartment owner) **takes a third." But others say: "The lower takes three fourths, and the upper takes a fourth."'**

Rabbah said: 'Uphold (the rulings) **of Rabbi Nossan, for he is a judge, and he plumbs the depths of the law.'** He (Rabbi Nossan) **reasons: To what degree does the upper one** (apartment) **devalue the lower one? A third. Therefore, it** (the upper apartment) **can lay claim to a third.**

MISHNAH FOUR: *The Olive Press, the Unstable Tree or Wall, and the Worker's Wages*

Similarly, (in the case where) **an olive press is built into** (a cavern carved out of a) **rock, and a garden is** (planted) **on top** (of the roof of the cavern), **and it** (the roof of the cavern, partially) **caved in** (creating a hole between the roof of the cavern, partially) **caved in** (creating a hole between the rooftop garden and the lower level olive press), **the owner of the garden may come down and sow below** (on the floor of the cavern near the olive press), **until he** (the olive press owner) **repairs** (the roof, literally, builds a dome) over **his olive press chamber.**

If a wall or a tree fell into the public domain and caused damage, he (the owner of the wall or the tree) **is not liable to pay.** (But) **if they** (the authorities) **gave him a set time to cut down the tree or take down the wall, and one of them** (the wall or the tree) **fell within the given time, he** (the owner) **is not liable. If** (one of them fell) **after time was up, he is liable.**

Someone whose wall was close to his neighbor's garden, and it (the wall) **collapsed** (into the garden), **and he** (the garden's owner) **said to him** (the wall's owner), **'Move your stones,' and he** (the wall's owner) **replied to him** (the garden's owner), **'They** (the stones) **are yours** (to keep for the trouble I caused you, so you move them away),' **we do not listen to him** (the wall's owner). **In a case where he** (the garden's owner) **accepted** (the proposal to clear the stones as payment for taking possession of them), **and he** (the wall's owner then changed his mind and) **said to him** (the garden's owner), **'Here are your wages** (offering cash instead of the stones)**, and I will take** (back what is) **mine** (my stones),**'** **we do not listen to him.**

One who hires a worker to work with him in straw or stubble, and he (the worker) **said to him** (the employer), **'Give me my wages,' and he** (the employer) **replied, 'Take what you did** (the straw you cut for me) **as your wages,' we do not listen to him. In a case where the worker accepts** (the straw)**, and he** (the employer changed his mind and) **said to him** (the worker), **'Here is your wage** (in cash) **and I will take** (back what is) **mine** (the straw),**' we do not listen to him.**

GEMARA

(How much of) **a cave-in** (occurred)? **Rav says: 'A majority** (of the roof).**'; Shmuel says: 'Four** (handbreadths).**' Rav says: '(Where) a majority** (of the roof caved in the owner of the garden may transfer his entire garden down below), **but** (where) **four** (handbreadths caved in) **he may not, for a person can plant half below and half above. But Shmuel says: 'Where only four** (hands-breadth caved in, he may move his entire garden below) **as a person does not plant half below and half above.' And it was necessary** (to repeat Rav and Shmuel's dispute from the first mishnah), **for if we would have taught** (this dispute only concerning the case of) **the apartment** (and not regarding the garden case we might have thought that) **in that case Shmuel issues his ruling because people do not usually live a little bit** here and a little bit there (in two separate places), **but with regard to sowing** (a garden), **people do sow a little bit here and a little bit there.** (Therefore) **one could say that** (in this current case of the garden, but not in the case of the apartment, that) **Rav admits that his** (Shmuel's approach) **is correct. But if it** (the dispute) **would have been mentioned in that case** (the garden), (we would have thought) **in that case Rav maintains his ruling** (that the owner of the garden above should only receive an area equivalent to the cave-in below, because people can sow in two places) **but here** (in the case of the apartment) **Rav admits to Shmuel's approach** (being correct, that even if only a small area of an apartment floor caved in, a person may move completely into the downstairs apartment because a person can not be expected to live on two floors). **So it was necessary** (to state their opinions, even though similar, in both cases).

'If they (the authorities) **gave him a set time to cut down the tree or take down the wall.' How much time does the court give? Rabbi Yochanan said: 'Thirty days.'**

(As the mishnah stated): **Someone whose wall was close to his neighbor's garden, and it** (the wall) **collapsed** (into the garden) **etc.**

Since the latter part of the mishnah declares 'Here are your wages,' we are dealing with a case where he (the garden owner) **had already removed them** (the stones). **The reason** (the garden owner may keep the stones as payment) **is that he removed them** (already), **but if he had not yet removed them, he may not** (keep the stones). **Why is this so? His field** (his property) **should have acquired the stones for him** (even if he had not removed them), for Rabbi Yose bar Rabbi Chanina maintained that 'A person's courtyard acquires for him without his knowledge.' These words (of Rabbi Chanina's) apply in a case where he (the owner of the object) intended to transfer ownership to him (the owner of the courtyard). But in the present case, he was just evading his request (when he told the garden owner that he could keep the stones if he cleared them; he had hoped to evade the courtyard acquiring the stones for its owner, so that he would have time to remove them himself).

(The Gemara quotes the next part of the mishnah): 'One who hires a worker to work with him in straw or stubble, and he (the worker) said to him (the employer), "Give me my wages," and he (the employer) replied, "Take what you did (the straw you cut for me) as your wages," we do not listen to him. In a case where the worker accepts (the straw), and he (the employer changed his mind and) said to him (the worker), "Here is your wage (in cash) and I will take (back what is) mine (the straw)," we do not listen to him.'

It was necessary (to rule on both cases, the case of the stones in the garden and the case of the straw as payment) for if it (the mishnah) had taught only the first case (where the wall collapsed into a neighbor's garden) then when he (the wall's owner) says, 'Keep it (the stones, if you clear them away),' we do not listen to him (when he says he would like to pay the garden owner in stones rather than money) as they do not have a wage agreement between them (because the owner of the garden has no payment due him until he agrees to remove the stones and does so; therefore, the type of payment is not yet fixed). But here (in the case of straw, offered as payment for a day's work in the field), **where there is a wage agreement between them** (the employer owes the laborer payment), **one might say we do listen to him** (the employer) **for as the popular saying goes, 'From one who is in your debt, collect even bran'** (do not pass up the opportunity for any form of payment). **And if it** (the mishnah) **would have taught the principle here** (of accepting straw as wages, and omitted discussing the case of stones as wages), (one might have thought) **here, once he** (the worker) **accepted** (straw as payment), **we do not listen to the employer** (if he changes his mind) **because the employer owes the laborer payment** (and he accepted the straw), **but here** (or rather, there, in the case of the garden owner) **he is owed no payment** (by the stones' owner); **therefore, one might suggest listening to him** (the stones' owner when he changed his mind and wanted to keep the stones), **so it was necessary** (for both cases to be discussed).

(We learned in the mishnah: When the employer says to the employee, 'Take what you did,') **We do not listen to him** (the employer, if he offers to pay the laborer in straw instead of in cash). **But we learned in a baraisa that we do listen to him. Rav Nachman said: 'This is not a contradiction for here** (in the mishnah) **it is his** (it is the employer's straw the employee refuses) **and here** (in the baraisa) **it is someone else's** (it is from someone else's field).'

Rabbah said to Rav Nachman: In his own, what is the reason (why, when he works in the employer's field does the mishnah forbid the employer from paying the worker in straw)? **Because** (the worker) **can say to him** (the employer), **'You are liable to pay my wages** (in money).' **In another's field, he** (the employer) **is also liable to pay**

the worker's wages (and, therefore, he can demand a cash payment). **For it was taught in a baraisa: 'If one** (an employer) **hires a worker** (to work) **in his own** (field), **and instead he shows him a neighbor's** (field to work in), **he must pay him** (the worker) **wages in full and then collect from the owner** (of the other property) **what benefit he gave him** (whatever the owner owes him for). **Rather, said Rav Nachman, there is no contradiction** (between the mishnah and the baraisa) **for here** (the mishnah) **is dealing with his own** (straw, payment in straw collected from employer's field), **and here** (the baraisa) **is dealing with ownerless** (straw, payment in straw collected from an ownerless field).

Rava challenged Rav Nachman (using another baraisa): **'An ownerless object found by a worker belongs to him.' When is this? When the employer either said to him, 'Weed for me today' or 'Dig for me today,' but if he** (the employer) **said to him, 'Work for me the entire day,' than the find belongs to the employer.**

Rather, said Rav Nachman:'There is no contradiction. Here (in the mishnah), **the case is one of lifting** (acquiring the straw in an ownerless field on the employer's behalf), **and, here** (in the baraisa), **the case is one of watching** (or standing guard over the ownerless straw on the employer's behalf).'

Rabbah said: 'Watching (standing guard over) **ownerless property is debated by the Rabbis of the** Mishnah. **We learned in a mishnah** (*Shekalim* 4:1): **"Those who guard the aftergrowth of the *Shemitta*** (Sabbatical year) **take their wages from the Temple treasury. Rabbi Yose said: 'One who wishes, donates** (his time) **and guards** (or watches) **without being paid.' They** (the Rabbis) **said to him: 'So**

you say, but then the offerings will not come from the community.'" Are they not arguing about this (whether merely watching an ownerless object can effect its acquisition)? **The *Tanna Kamma*** (literally, the first of the Rabbis to offer an opinion in the mishnah) **contends that watching an ownerless object can effect its acquisition, and if he** (the watchman) **is paid** (for his work), **yes** (than the aftergrowth belongs to the community). **But if** (he is) **not** (paid, than) **no** (it does not belong to the community, for the volunteer watchman will acquire the ownerless produce for himself). **But Rabbi Yose contends that watching an ownerless object cannot effect its acquisition** (so the Temple need not pay the watchman, he cannot acquire it anyway). (In such a circumstance) **when the community goes and brings it** (the crop), **then the community acquires it. And then what** (is the meaning of) **do 'you say?' This is what they** (the Rabbis) **said to him** (Rabbi Yose): **'From your words to our words** (based upon your opinion that the guard need not be paid, and our opinion that watching can effect acquisition) **the *omer*** (barley offering on the second day of Pesah) **and the *shtei halechem*** (offering of two wheat loaves on Shavuot) **will not come from the community.'**

Rava said: 'No. Everyone (Rabbi Yose and the Rabbis) **agrees that watching ownerless property can effect its acquisition** (and so the watchman does acquire the produce), **but here they argue over whether** (having acquired them) **he** (the watchman) **will hand them over to the community unreservedly** (wholeheartedly). **The Rabbis maintain that we pay him a wage, because if not, we are concerned he may not hand them** (the crops) **over unreservedly. But Rabbi Yose contends that we are not worried about his handing them over unreservedly. And**

what is the meaning of 'you say.' This is what they (the Rabbis) **said to him** (Rabbi Yose): **'From your words to our words** (based upon your opinion that the guard need not be paid, and our opinion) **that the worker will not hand it over unreservedly the omer and the shtei halechem will not come from the community.'**

Some say that Rava said that everyone (Rabbi Yose and the Rabbis) **agree that watching ownerless property does not effect its acquisition** (and so the watchman does not acquire the produce), **but here they argue over whether we need to worry about hoodlums** (who will take the produce by force). **The Tanna Kamma maintains that the Sages decreed the watchman be paid four** *zuzim* (the *zuz* was a coin used in Talmudic times) **so that the hoodlums would hear** (that the crop belongs to the Temple) **and not take it. But Rabbi Yose contends that the Sages did not promulgate this decree** (for they were not fearful that hoodlums would take the growth). **And what is the meaning of 'you say.' This is what they** (the Rabbis) **said to him** (Rabbi Yose): **'From your words to our words** (based upon your position that the worker is not paid, he will not give it over whole heartedly) **so the omer and the shtei halechem will not come from the community.' And when Ravin came** (to Babylonia from the Land of Israel) **he taught in the name of Rabbi Yochanan that Rabbi Yose and the Rabbis argued over whether we need worry about hoodlums.**

MISHNAH FIVE: *Placing or Storing Privately Owned Objects in the Public Domain*

(In the case where) **one places manure in the public domain, the placer places, and the fertilizer fertilizes** (immediately after the manure has been placed in the public domain, so no obstruction is created). **One may not soak clay in the public domain** (for the purpose of making bricks) **nor may one make bricks** (in the public domain, as the drying of the bricks obstructs the public domain for a long time). **However, one may knead clay in the public domain, if it is not for making bricks** (as just preparing the clay for mortar creates an obstruction for a brief time). (In a case where) **one builds in the public domain, the stone bringer brings, and the builder builds** (using the stones immediately). **But if he** (the builder) **caused damages** (because he stored materials in the public domain), **he pays for the damage caused. Rabban Shimon ben Gamliel maintains: 'The builder may even begin setting up his building materials** (up to) **thirty days** (before).'

GEMARA

Shall we say our mishnah does not rule in accord with Rabbi Yehudah? For it was taught in a baraisa: 'Rabbi Yehudah said: "In the season when manure is taken out, a person may place his manure in the public domain and pile it up every thirty days so that it will be crushed by the feet of people and the feet of animals, for Joshua distributed the Land (to the tribes of Israel) **with this stipulation.'''**

(No)**, you can even say that Rabbi Yehudah** (agrees with the mishnah)**, for Rabbi Yehudah admits that if** (someone caused) **damage** (through his actions, he is) **liable to pay** (for the damage). **But we have learned a mishnah** (which contradicts this assumption): **'Rabbi Yehudah admits in** (the case of) **a Hanukkah lamp** (left in the street) **one is not liable** (to pay for damage the lamp's flame causes because) **he acts with permission** (in fulfilling the rabbinic commandment to publicize the Hanukkah miracle).' **Must this not mean by permission of the court? No, by permission of a mitzva.**

But it was taught in a baraisa: '(Concerning) **all these things about which the Sages said one may ruin the public domain, if he causes damage, he is obliged to make restitution** (for what he damages). **But Rabbi Yehudah exempts him from making restitution.' Rather, clearly our mishnah does not follow Rabbi Yehudah's** (view). **Declared Abaye: 'Rabbi Yehudah, Rabban Shimon ben Gamliel and Rabbi Shimon all held that in every case where the Rabbis gave an individual permission** (to use the public domain), **and he caused damage, he is exempt from liability.' That Rabbi Yehudah held this way** (that he does not hold the damager liable to pay) **was proven above** (in the baraisa). (That) **Rabban Shimon ben Gamliel** (does not hold the damager liable to pay is proven) **by our mishnah where he said, 'The builder may even begin setting up his building materials** (up to) **thirty days** (before).' (That) **Rabbi Shimon** (does not hold the damager liable to pay is as) **we learned** (in another) **mishnah: 'If a person**

places an oven in an upper story, there must be beneath it (an extra) **layer of plaster three handbreadths thick; but in the case of a stove, one handbreadths; and if he caused damage** (despite taking this precaution), **he must pay damages.** (But regarding this matter) **Rabbi Shimon says that the Sages did not mention all these measurements,** (for any reason) **other than** (to teach us that) **if it caused damage, the owner is not obliged to pay.'**

The Rabbis taught in a baraisa: 'When the quarrier delivers (the stone) **to the chiseler, the chiseler is liable** (for any damage to the stone or that the stone may do); **when the chiseler delivers** (the stone) **to the donkey driver, the donkey driver is liable; when the donkey driver delivers** (the stone) **to the carrier, the carrier is liable; when the carrier delivers** (the stone) **to the builder, the builder is liable; when the builder delivers** (the stone) **to the bricklayer, the bricklayer is liable. But if he** (the bricklayer) **sets the stone in the row** (completing the bricklaying process), **and it** (fell and) **caused damage, all are liable.' But it was taught in another baraisa: 'The last one is liable, and all the others are exempt.' There is no contradiction. In this case** (the second baraisa), (the individuals were) **hired** (separately to do their individual jobs); **in that case** (the first baraisa), (they were) **contracted** (as a group).

MISHNAH SIX: *Whose Garden Is It?*

(In the case where) **there are two gardens** (each owned by a different person), **one above the other, and vegetables** (grow out of the cliffside) **between them** (on the vertical drop between the two gardens), **Rabbi Meir rules: 'They** (the vegetables) **belong to the upper** (garden).' **Rabbi Yehudah rules: 'They** (the vegetables) **belong to the lower** (garden).' **Argued Rabbi Meir: 'If the** (owner of the) **upper** (garden) **wants to remove his dirt** (down to the level of the lower garden), **there would be no vegetables** (growing on the cliffside; indeed, there would be no cliff).' **Responded Rabbi Yehudah: 'If the** (owner of the) **lower** (garden) **wanted to fill his garden up** (with soil) **there would be no vegetables** (growing on the cliffside; indeed, there would be no cliff). **Then, Rabbi Meir said: 'Since each of them can protest the other's ownership, we establish where the vegetables get their nourishment from.' Rabbi Shimon declared: 'Whatever the** (owner of the) **upper** (garden) **can reach and pick by stretching out his hand belongs to him, and the rest belongs to the** (owner of the) **lower** (garden).'

GEMARA

Rava states: 'With regard to the roots, no one argues, they belong to the upper (garden). **What do they argue about it? With regard to the part that is seen** (the branches or foliage, and the vegetables or fruits growing outside the soil). **R Meir says: "Throw the part above ground after the roots** (the foliage and produce is nurtured by the roots, and so is owned by the owner of the upper garden)." **Rabbi Yehudah argues: "We do not say throw the part that is seen after the roots** (and so it belongs to the lower garden owner)."' **They** (Rabbi Meir and Rabbi Yehudah) **are consistent with their approach elsewhere, for we learned in a baraisa: 'That which sprouts out of a** (tree's) **trunk or roots,** (the tree having been sold by the landowner to a buyer who bought just the tree, but not the land it is on), **it** (the new shoot off the tree) **belongs to the owner of the land** (rather than to the owner of the tree) **according to Rabbi Meir. But Rabbi Yehudah says that which sprouts from the trunk belongs to the owner of the** (tree) **trunk, and** (that which grows from the roots, such as a) **a shoot from the roots, belongs to the owner of the land.'**

And we also learned a similar argument in a (different) **baraisa concerning the laws of** *orla*: **'A tree which sprouts from the trunk or the roots is subject to** (the laws of) **orla, according to Rabbi Meir. Rabbi Yehudah says that if it sprouts from the trunk, it is not obligated in orla, but** (if it sprouts) **from the roots it is subject to the laws** (of orla).'

And both (cases) **are necessary** (to mention). **For if you would discuss** (only) **the first case** (the sale of the tree), (you might have reasoned that) **in this case Rabbi Yehudah ruled this way because it is a monetary case** (in monetary cases he would rule according to the letter of the law as with two parties financially dependent upon the court's ruling, we need to rule exactly), **but in** (a case of) **orla,**

which is a matter of (ritual) **prohibition** (where leniency may be an option, as two parties are not involved in a dispute), **one could argue that he** (Rabbi Yehudah) **would agree with Rabbi Meir. And if we had only discussed the dispute** (as it related to orla), (you might have reasoned that) in this case **Rabbi Meir ruled this way** (stringently in the case of a ritual prohibition), **but in the other he would agree with Rabbi Yehudah. So it was necessary** (to discuss both cases).

Rabbi Shimon said (in our mishnah): **'Whatever the upper one** (garden owner) **can reach by stretching out his hands is his, and the rest belongs to the lower** (garden owner).' **They said in the academy of Rabbi Yannai: 'As long as he does not have to overstretch.' Rav Anan posed a question, and some say Rabbi Yirmiya** (asked it): **'If the owner of the upper garden can reach the foliage, but not the roots, or if he can reach its roots but not its foliage, what** (is the law)**?' Let it go unanswered. Ephraim, the** scribe, **who was a disciple of Resh Lakish said in the name of Resh Lakish that the law is in accord with the view of Rabbi Shimon. They reported the ruling to King Shapur who said to them: 'Rabbi Shimon should be praised.'**

EPILOGUE

A long-standing rabbinic tradition dictates that we should always end on a positive note, looking hopefully towards the future. In this case, I conclude with another story about trees and with a blessing. In the eleventh chapter of tractate *Sanhedrin*, we learn: "All Israelites have a portion in the World to Come, as it is said: 'And Your people are all righteous; they shall possess the land forever; they are a branch of My own planting, the work of My hands, wherein I may glory (*Isaiah* 60:21).'" What does it mean to be a branch planted by God? The following passage from tractate *Ta'anit* provides an answer and offers me a way of thanking you for the time and concentration you put into studying this book:

> When they (Rabbi Yitzchak and Rav Nachman) **were parting from each other, he** (Rav Nachman) **said to him** (Rabbi Yitzchak), **'Bless me, Master.' He** (Rabbi Yitzchak) **responded: 'I will tell you a parable. To what is this** (the matter of your blessing) **comparable? To a person who was walking in the desert, hungry, tired, and thirsty. He found a tree whose fruits were sweet and whose shade was pleasant, that had a stream of water passing under it. He ate of its fruit, drank of its water, and sat in its shade. When he wanted to go, he said** (to the tree that had given so much to him): **"O tree, O tree, with what shall I bless you? If I say to you may your fruit be sweet, it is already sweet. If I say to you may your**

149

shade be pleasant, it is already pleasant. If I say to you may you have water passing under you, water already passes under you. Rather, let it be (God's will) that all the shoots that are planted from cuttings taken from you will be just like you." And so it is with you (Rav Nachman). With what shall I bless you? If I bless you with Torah (knowledge), behold, you already have it. If I bless you with wealth, you already have that it. If I bless you with children, you already have them. Rather, may it be (God's will) that your children will be just like you.'

SUGGESTED READINGS

Complete Talmud Translations with Commentary

The Mishnah: *Bava Metzia*, with commentary by Rabbi Pinchas Kehati. Trans. Edward Levin (The Jewish Agency, Department of Jewish Education, 1994).

Clear and comprehensive commentary on the Mishnah written by Rabbi Pinchas Kehati, including a brief summary of the Gemara's discussion of each mishnah.

The Soncino Talmud. Ed. Rabbi Dr. Isadore Epstein (London: Soncino Press, 1935).

The first complete English translation of the Talmud, with minimal commentary, is an excellent reference for the English speaker.

The Talmud: *Bava Metzia*. Steinsaltz Edition, Vol. 6, Part 6 (New York: Random House, 1993); *The Talmud, Tractate Bava Metzia*. Schottenstein Edition (New York: Mesorah Publications, 1994).

Both the Steinsaltz and Schottenstein translations have revolutionized Talmud study by inserting translations of the Talmudic text into the midst of a running commentary. The reader feels as if the author is sitting across the table from him, engaging him or her in a one-on-one study session. Additional mini-essays summarizing and explaining disputes between the classical commentators further the reader's understanding and provide him or her with access to generations of Talmudic commentary and responsa.

Stories of the Talmudic Sages

Biographical sketches of the lives of rabbinic contributors to the Talmud.)

Bader, Gershom. *The Encyclopedia of Talmudic Sages.* (Northvale, New Jersey: Jason Aaronson Publishers, 1993).

Morganstern, Benjamin. *A Companion to Pirke Avot.* (Jerusalem: Gefen Press, 1983).

Wiesel, Elie. *Sages and Dreamers: Biblical, Talmudic and Hasidic Portraits and Legends.* (New York: Summit Books, 1991).

Interpretations of Talmudic Passages

(Interpretations and explanations of selected Talmudic passages, giving the

reader a more in-depth look at Talmudic ethics, as well as providing some insight into the personalities of the Talmudic sages.)

Katz, Michael & Schwartz, Gershon. *Swimming in the Sea of Talmud: Lessons for Everyday Living.* (Philadelphia: JPS, 1998).

Levinas, Emmanuel. *Beyond the Verse.* Trans. Gary D. Mole (Bloomington: Indiana University Press, 1994).

Idem. *Nine Talmudic Reading by Emmanuel Levinas.* Trans. Annette Aronowicz (Bloomington: Indiana University Press, 1994).

Licht, Chaim. *Ten Legends of the Sages: The Image of the Sage in Rabbinic Literature.* (Hoboken, New Jersey: KTAV, 1995).

Schneerson, Menachem Mendel. *Beacons on the Talmud's Sea: Analysis of Passages from the Talmud and Issues of Halachah.* Adapted from the Works of the Lubavitcher Rebbe, Rabbi Menachem M. Schneerson, in English. (Brooklyn, New York: 1997).

Stone, Ira F. *Reading Levinas/Reading Talmud: An Introduction.* (Philadelphia: JPS, 1998).

The Process of Learning the Talmud

Heilman, Samuel. *The Gate Behind the Wall: A Pilgrimage to Jerusalem.*(Jerusalem: JPS, 1984).

During a sabbatical, the author attempts to gain insight into the Jewish value of textual study. This journey leads him through various venues for Talmudic learning, with Jerusalem's diverse neighborhoods as a backdrop.

Patai, Joseph. *The Middle Gate: A Hungarian Jewish Boyhood.* (Jerusalem: JPS, 1994).

This book tells the story of a year in the author's childhood spent studying the tractate *Bava Metzia* after school. The stories of the tractate are interwoven with the harsh life of Jewish Hungary.

General Talmudic Knowledge

Parry, Aaron. *The Complete Idiot's Guide to the Talmud.* (Alpha Books, 2004).

A basic overview of Talmudic concepts in simple language, with a number of topics explored in greater detail.